Selling
Vision

The
X ➡ XY ➡ Y
Formula
for Driving Results
by Selling Change

Lou Schachter
and Rick Cheatham

New York   Chicago   San Francisco   Lisbon   London
Madrid   Mexico City   Milan   New Delhi   San Juan
Seoul   Singapore   Sydney   Toronto

1 2 3 4 5 6 7 8 9 0   QFR/QFR   1 2 1 0 9 8 7 6

ISBN   978-1-259-64217-3
MHID   1-259-64217-8

e-ISBN 978-1-259-64218-0
e-MHID   1-259-64218-6

Library of Congress Cataloging-in-Publication Data

Names: Schachter, Lou, author. I Cheatham, Rick, author.
Title: Selling vision : the X-XY-Y formula for driving results by selling change / Lou Schachter and Rick Cheatham.
Description: New York : McGraw-Hill, [2016] I Includes index.
Identifiers: LCCN 2015051011I ISBN 9781259642173 (alk. paper) I ISBN 1259642178 (alk. paper)
Subjects: LCSH: Selling. I Sales management. I Organizational change.
Classification: LCC HF5438.25 .S323 2016 I DDC 658.8/1—dc23
    LC record available at http://lccn.loc.gov/2015051011

McGraw-Hill Education books are available at special quantity discounts to use as premiums and sales promotions or for use in corporate training programs. To contact a representative, please visit the Contact Us page at www.mhprofessional.com.

To Wayne and Jen

Contents

PART 1

A New Logic for Sales Transformation

CHAPTER 1

Time for Change

The Moment of Clarity

You have built a beautiful business. But lately, waves of change are slowly eroding its base. Until now you have held back the damage by reinforcing the foundation. Then one day the realization hits you: you must move the whole structure, or it will be swept away, like a sandcastle on the beach.

For so many of us, that is precisely how it feels when the market for what our company sells stops growing. Or when a newly emerged competitor (who seemed like an irrelevant gnat just a year ago) releases an offering that is beginning to transform the marketplace. Advances in technology are making new products possible or making it cheaper to produce the old products.

Sometimes the trouble occurs because our customers are changing. The customers may be confronting a shock in their own market (e.g., contractions in electronics retailing, fluctuating oil prices) and are less able to make their traditional purchases. Or the customers' buying behaviors are changing. Often what is changing is who is doing the buying within each customer organization. New buyers bring different purchasing criteria with them.

The drivers of change can also be positive. A new, more attractive segment of customers might be emerging. Our colleagues in engineering or product development may be ready to release some major innovations. We may have discovered that a few of our salespeople have become very successful selling in a different way, or to different buyers, or to different types of companies.

Whatever the cause, the moment will come. How you respond will determine your personal success, that of your customers, and to a great extent that of your company.

It's pretty common to confront changes like those above and deny them, at least initially. Successful selling requires a great deal of optimism, so too often sellers and sales leaders dismiss early signs of the need to change as unnecessary negativity. Optimism alone, many sales leaders facing change believe, will win the day. But in this case optimism is just another word for denial. While it's natural to be in that space for a while, too much time there, or too much commitment to past success, can be deadly.

"Creative Destruction"

It's not so easy to be great forever. By most accounts, only 2 of the 11 companies cited by Jim Collins in *Good to Great* are still "great" today. Using another measure, the length of time that a corporation spends in the S&P 500 has dropped from 61 years in 1958 to just 18 years today. Richard Foster and Sarah Kaplan, in *Creative Destruction*, explain that the companies that perform best over a 10- to 15-year period typically have strong cultures and meticulous bureaucracies. But it is exactly these qualities that make them stall out after that period.

Foster and Kaplan propose that success comes not from continuity but instead from discontinuity. They advocate the constant destruction and re-creation of companies to remain competitive. They argue that successful companies are those that are as dynamic as the market itself. Foster wrote in an earlier book that during periods of technological discontinuities, "Attackers, rather than defenders, have the economic advantage." This is the situation we see so often today, where new entrants deploy new technologies to disrupt established markets. Legacy players are left facing the moment of clarity we described above.

High-performing salespeople often naturally figure out the right things to do in times of disruption; or because they are so skilled, they can get by for longer by ignoring the need for change. Low performers often become victims in times of change, blaming bad leadership, misguided efforts by other departments, and irrational customer demands. Fortunately, the core of most sales organizations is populated by optimists, but they often don't know what to do when confronted by change and can easily fall into a state of denial.

Who is responsible for staying ahead of the market? Maybe it's the R&D folks; maybe it should be owned by marketing and product development. You can argue that it's the CEO's responsibility. But here's one thing that is true: the chief sales officer who takes responsibility for staying ahead of marketplace changes (rather than becoming a victim of them) is the CSO who will likely become a CEO.

That Sinking Feeling

The need for sales transformation is presenting itself in different ways to people, depending on their roles. Here is how the world looks today to three real sales professionals we have met (names and identifying details have been changed).

The Lost Edge

Jack has been selling for over 20 years. He has spent most of his career at two companies and has been successful at both. In fact, he quickly moved from key accounts to area sales manager. Within the region, the entire sales team was delighted to see one of their own, *a guy that really gets it*, in charge for a change. Today Jack is back in the selling role and struggling to meet his targets. What happened?

Jack failed at the sales manager role, as many successful salespeople do, because he was unable to provide meaningful direction to his team. He had good intentions, but he tried to get others to sell the way he had, which was somewhat unique, given his particular personality and experiences. For a while he was seen as a good manager because the person he replaced was not suited to the role, but eventually the numbers caught up with Jack. He was not able to lead his team to growth.

Jack was discouraged by the chain of events, and as we noted earlier, he is back as a salesperson and struggling. Is it because he's been depressed by his recent experiences? Perhaps. But more likely, Jack's failure at sales management and difficulty selling today is a result of falling out of sync with the changing marketplace.

Jack—like many other salespeople today—is feeling that he has lost his edge. The activities and behaviors that once worked for him no longer get results. He is questioning whether he can be successful again.

Back to Basics

Joan is a sales manager. Her sales team, which is very experienced, has shown some improvement recently, but really it has continued to struggle since the global financial crisis many years ago. There has been very slight growth, but it has often come at the expense of margins.

Customers of Joan's company, which we will call Allstar, have shown an increased resistance to Allstar's pricing model. These customers are less interested than they once were in paying a premium, particularly given that newer competitors have similar offerings at lower prices.

Joan feels that the market has not really changed. She believes her team has become complacent, and even lazy. In response, she has pushed harder to drive and measure specific sales activities. She is focusing on five measures: call volume, meetings scheduled, opportunities identified, proposals submitted, and referrals generated. While this has had some positive impact on sales, it has also added a lot of noise to the CRM: leads that are not qualified, meetings that don't drive sales, and opportunities that never close.

Joan knows there are people in her organization who are pushing for a major change in how Allstar goes to market. Joan tries to build consensus around the idea that no big change is necessary. She aligns herself with others opposed to change, and she shares examples of how any significant level of change would negatively impact her customers. In management meetings, Joan recommends that the sales organization stay focused on internal issues, such as conflicts with the marketing department, customer service issues, and a quality problem in a recent product release. Fixing those, Joan argues, is the key to growth.

In summary, Joan believes that one more quarter is all she needs to prove that a big change is not necessary.

Horror Show

Helen has spent her whole career in the same organization and has been in her sales leader role for several years. As a salesperson, she had the fastest success of anyone in the history of the organization. She is well loved both by customers, who value her intelligence, and by her employees, who value her passion and compassion.

Helen recently had a moment of clarity. Her team just posted a year-over-year decline, a first in her career. While also feeling accountable to her company and boss, Helen's primary reaction is one of having let the people on her team down. "They trusted me to make choices that protected their jobs," Helen thinks to herself. "I've got to figure out a way to fix this."

Helen finds it hard to put a finger on when the problems started. She isn't sure what she missed. What she feels is a great deal of uncertainty. It feels like the wind has blown open a door in a horror movie. For an instant everyone can't help but expect a serial killer on the other side. Helen tries to keep her emotions just this side of panic.

Helen knows she needs to fix the situation, but she does not know how.

Taking the Bird's-Eye View

For Jack, Joan, and Helen, these are highly uncertain times, as they are for the salespeople, sales managers, and sales leaders they stand in for. Most sales professionals have been in the same sticky situations as Jack, Joan, and Helen even if they haven't held the exact same roles. How many of us have not:

- Feared losing the skills that made us successful in the past?

- Hoped that increased activity levels will overcome decreasing performance?

- Experienced feelings of panic when a major realization sets in?

For every sales role, and for every negative emotion above, there is an answer. That answer requires looking at the situation from a higher vantage point and seeing it in the context of larger waves of change that are washing over all markets today. By reconfiguring our response to marketplace change, we can quickly shift from being a victim or lost soul to being a leader.

Charting the Course

This book is a road map to staying ahead of marketplace change. For sales leaders, it provides a path for transforming the sales organization. For sales managers, it describes how to inspire change in the behavior of salespeople. And for salespeople, it offers a new way of selling that will have a dramatic impact on success. Whichever role you are in, this book will provide you with immediate actions you can take and experiments you can conduct to find the right direction for your future efforts.

This book is about sales. It is also about change management. In fact, in many respects, sales today is essentially change management.

The book is organized into five parts. In Part 1, we propose a new logic for thinking about and executing major change in sales organizations—what we will refer to as sales transformations. In Part 2, we examine sales transformations from the customer's perspective, and we show how the customer's changing buying patterns suggest a particular way of focusing a sales transformation and selling activity. In Part 3, we focus on the perspective of salespeople and what they can do to sell change to their customers who are also going through transformations. In Part 4, we look at how sales leaders and sales managers can change the way selling works in their organizations. Finally, in Part 5, we highlight the pivotal moments that determine the success of major change initiatives in sales organizations.

CHAPTER 2

A New Way of Seeing Change

A number of books and papers have provided models for how companies' go-to-market approaches must adapt to change. We propose a simple model, where a company is in a shift from selling a lot of X and a little bit of something new called Y . . . to a lot of Y and much less of the X legacy offering, as shown in Figure 2.1.

X and Y can be what you sell or how you sell. What you sell may be shifting to radically new products or to radically new services. How you sell may involve new types of customers, new types of buyers within existing customer organizations, or new, fundamentally different selling approaches.

More specifically, some examples of the shift from X to Y can be:

- A change from selling on-premise software to offering cloud solutions

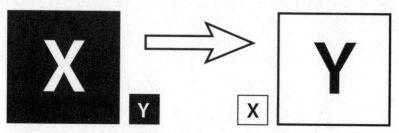

Figure 2.1   A shift from selling a lot of X and a little Y to less X and more Y.

- A shift in pricing models from an approach that requires significant up-front payments to one that is based on monthly subscriptions

- A change from selling equipment to leasing equipment

- A need to move from selling print advertising to digital advertising

- An effort to move salespeople from focusing on selling product features to selling the results the products will generate

- A change from selling to technical buyers to selling to C-suite buyers

- A shift from selling direct to selling through a channel (or the reverse)

- A change from selling the value of product features to selling the business impact of both products and ancillary services

Sometimes a new competitor introduces a Y offering into the X marketplace, and the big X players have no choice but to provide a Y alternative. This is what's happened in the cloud space.

But it's also happened to taxi companies, with the advent of Uber. Often though, companies figure out Y on their own, frequently in collaboration with one or more of their biggest customers.

Initially a company is selling a lot of X and a little bit of Y. It looks like the pie chart in Figure 2.2, if you were to measure revenue or volume.

Figure 2.2   Y represents a small share of revenue or volume.

Over time, if the strategy works, the idea is that the share of Y gets bigger. The progression looks something like that shown in Figure 2.3.

Figure 2.3   The share of revenue or volume from Y gets bigger.

As you can see, at the end, there comes a point when Y is no longer the new thing. Z emerges, and the process repeats itself.

What People Think Happens

Now let's look at how salespeople change as a result of a shift from selling X to selling Y. This is where it gets interesting. Let's start with what people think happens.

In the beginning, as shown in Figure 2.4, we have a few people selling Y, while most people are selling X. The diagram represents a normal distribution curve, showing the number of salespeople doing each type of selling.

Figure 2.4   In the beginning, there are just a few salespeople selling Y.

Then, the conventional wisdom says, over time you get more of your X salespeople to sell Y. This is usually where the hard work occurs, but with success, over time the progression is expected to look more like that shown in Figure 2.5. In time, as the figure shows, more and more salespeople sell Y. And at the end, before the cycle repeats, some of them start to sell Z.

Based on this model, sales leaders see it as their job to get more salespeople to sell Y more quickly. And that is hard. People resist change, especially big change. Typically, most salespeople who are told (or even taught) to start selling Y revert fairly quickly to selling X, as they always did. Sales leaders become frustrated by their inability to drive the shift they need. They often begin to wonder if they need new salespeople. They initiate an effort to recruit Y salespeople, often at great expense, and begin to let go X salespeople who can't make the shift to Y, which is also expensive.

Salespeople can be tremendously frustrated. Often executive discussions about a shift from X to Y can take months. Once a decision is reached, the leaders, who have had a significant period of time to consider and accept the change, now expect

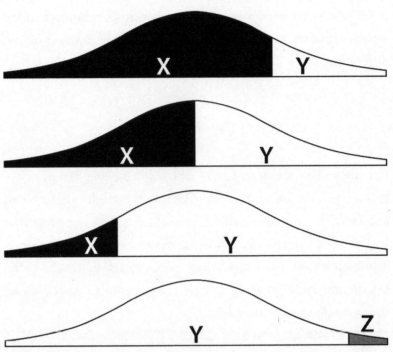

Figure 2.5   The conventional wisdom is that over time more salespeople switch from selling X to selling Y, and a few early adopters ultimately begin to sell Z.

salespeople to commit to it fully as soon as it is announced. Typically, salespeople, who have heard many big announcements over the years, wait things out to see if the change will stick, since so many before it have not.

Sales managers are often stuck in the middle between sales representatives who resist the change from X to Y and executives who insist upon it. The sales managers, themselves, often have mixed feelings about the new approach and are torn between being candid about their doubts and feeling an obligation to display confidence about the new direction.

There is a better way. Sales professionals who find themselves in this situation will benefit from looking at the situation differently.

What Really Happens

Driving a sales transformation—or even just being part of one—gets a whole lot easier when you realize the model above is not accurate. The shift from selling X to selling Y does not occur that way. It's not a binary event, where you turn off X and turn on Y. Thinking it's like a switch is what creates frustration for so many sales leaders and what creates resistance from salespeople and confusion in sales managers.

Let's look again at how salespeople change as a result of a shift from selling X to selling Y. What really happens is that in the beginning, as shown in Figure 2.6, we have a very few people selling purely Y, while most people are selling X, and a few are selling a combination we'll refer to as XY. That is, they are continuing to sell X while also selling Y. That is what happens in real life.

There will always be a few pure Y sellers (often new to the organization, sometimes from another firm that sold purely Y, or perhaps part of the original effort to introduce Y), but most people selling Y will still be selling a fair amount of X too. The salespeople are sometimes selling both X and Y at the same time; sometimes they are selling to their customers a combination solution that includes both X and Y.

The recognition of the XY combination is the key to understanding sales transformation. Over time, as you see on the

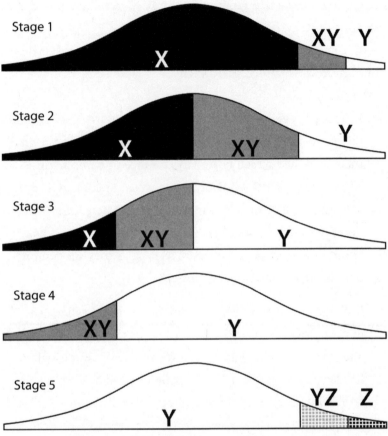

Figure 2.6   On the transition from selling X to selling Y,
salespeople go through a transition where they sell both X and Y.

distribution curves in Figure 2.6, salespeople do shift to selling Y
exclusively. But they only do that after a period of selling both X
and Y simultaneously.

The most critical element of making a sales transformation
successful is describing what it looks like to sell X and Y at the
same time or to sell XY combinations. It is not, as most sales
leaders wrongly assume today, simply defining Y and how to
sell it. Nor is it getting people to switch from X to Y. The key is

getting them to switch from selling only X to selling X and Y at the same time.

In our experience, Stage 2 is the critical moment that determines success or failure. Here's why:

- In Stage 1, you have a few of the original pure-Y sellers, and you have some XY sellers, who have likely figured out on their own how to sell both ways at once or combinations. These are typically some of your best salespeople who are also agile and always looking for the next new thing. They don't need much guidance. They figure out what works and adopt new approaches quickly, as long as they see genuinely positive reactions from customers.

- In Stage 2, you actually have to work to get X sellers (the majority of your historically successful salespeople) to adopt the XY selling approach. That is hard, and it's made harder by trying to get X salespeople to sell Y. We have worked with dozens of the largest and most admired sales forces in the world as they execute sales transformations. What we have discovered is that instead of driving X salespeople to sell Y, what successful sales leaders do is get X salespeople to begin selling XY. Later, we'll go deeper into exactly how to do that. But if you don't get Stage 2 right, you won't see the later stages. You'll likely be looking for a new job. If you do get Stage 2 right, the later stages will take care of themselves, to a great extent.

As we go forward in our discussions, we'll talk about the difference between two ways of seeing sales transformation:

The Traditional Approach:

X → Y

The *Selling Vision* Approach:

X → XY → Y

Table 2.1 provides an easy way to see how we will use these terms throughout this book.

Reference	What it means
X	What you have been selling—or how you have been selling.
Y	What you want to be selling—or how you want to be selling—in the future.
XY	Selling both X and Y at the same time, either simultaneously or in combination.
X-to-Y	A change from selling X to selling Y.
X→Y	A change from selling X directly to selling Y without an intended XY period.
X→XY→Y	A change from selling X to selling Y, but with a clearly defined period in which you are selling both X and Y.

Table 2.1   Terminology

CHAPTER 3

Examples of
X-to-Y Change

What does an X-to-Y change look like? Let's look at some examples. Each of these stories is based on a company we have worked with, but identifying details have been changed.

First we'll look at two companies that struggled with their transformation. Then we'll examine two more successful examples.

Bridgewater

This first example is about a company that failed to define the XY phase clearly enough.

Bridgewater is a U.S. professional services firm that is a broker for health insurance. Its clients are Fortune 500 companies. In business for close to 100 years, it is in a constant battle with its nearest competitor for the #1 or #2 position in its industry. Over several years, Bridgewater's margins began to decline, as it lowered its bids to maintain business in a fiercely competitive landscape.

A few years ago, the board of directors brought in a new CEO from outside the company to lead Bridgewater to a new era of success. For several years, the company's revenue had been flat or declining, and Bridgewater needed a turnaround. The new CEO, whom we'll call Mark Wellington, fairly quickly assembled a new vision for the company. Not only would it offer health insurance brokerage services; it would also be a consultant to its clients who were struggling to adapt to the quickly changing healthcare environment in the United States. There were small pockets in the organization where this work had developed naturally. Now it was time to expand the work to the bulk of its clients.

Wellington's perspective was that the shift to a more consultative approach would have three benefits: (1) it would create a new revenue stream that leveraged the firm's core competencies while being less price-sensitive, (2) it would reduce churn by providing clients added reasons to buy their health insurance through Bridgewater, and (3) it would position Bridgewater as a C-suite advisor to its clients. This vision of providing advice was the Y future that Wellington introduced to the organization.

Immediately, many top executives and several opinion-leading producers got on board. After going through several CEOs in a short period, many welcomed this new and clear strategy. But at the same time, many of the rank-and-file brokers were hesitant. They felt that Wellington's strategy would take Bridgewater into an area where the firm did not have well-defined expertise and work processes. Many people attracted to the insurance industry are naturally risk avoidant, and they saw many risks in Wellington's new strategy. The fact that Wellington came in from outside the firm did not help.

Wellington was not recommending a giant shift in the firm's strategy. In fact, his vision was always expressed as one of becoming the nation's premier health insurance broker and premier employee health advisor. So from a distance, it looks like he took both X (health insurance broker) and Y (healthcare consulting) into account. But let's see what happened.

Bridgewater fleshed out its plans, and then it hosted week-long workshops for its top 500 leaders and client managers. These events were expensive, well-orchestrated affairs. They combined elements of CEO town halls, sales kickoffs, and training programs. They included the voice of clients who articulated the need for Bridgewater to provide a more comprehensive offering. The training emphasized the need to expand each account manager's understanding of the businesses he or she served, delving much more deeply into the clients' strategies and describing the ways decisions about health insurance could impact those strategies. The sessions began with a well-articulated case for change. Participants were taught skills to help them manage relationships, understand the client mindset, become financially fluent, and talk to clients about health risks.

The sessions were enormously successful in that they were very well received, they were highly rated, and they energized the firm. Many people began pursuing the new approach with their clients and began to show early signs of success. However, the new revenue was slow to come. The advisory approach had long sales cycles, and there was a learning curve for the Bridgewater account managers. While the new approach was taking hold, revenue in the existing business continued to slide. A backlash grew among those who never supported the new strategy. In less than a year, Wellington was fired by the board of directors, and the new strategy was scrapped. A number of the champions of Wellington's vision later left the firm.

What happened? Why did Wellington's strategy fail so quickly? Would it have survived and succeeded if given more time? Here's what we believe occurred. While Wellington and his team always communicated a vision of both X (brokerage) and Y (consulting), they did not create the execution plan for selling both X and Y at once. As often happens, they assumed that since X was the legacy business, they should focus on what was new and different (Y) and emphasize how to do and sell that work in their presentations. What the rank-and-file missed was a sufficiently clear explanation of the XY phase. To them the message was "It is time to turn off X and turn on Y."

In our view, the transformation would have been more successful if Wellington had not tried to transform the whole firm at once. It would have been better to identify, say, 100 accounts to focus on initially and roll out the training only to those account managers. Once those accounts showed success, the training could be rolled out to the next 500 or 1,000.

Wellington obviously also failed in setting expectations with his board and top leaders. The firm was ready for fast results, and Wellington either underestimated or failed to explain the time it would take to execute the new approach. As a result, the clock ran out before he could show sufficient success.

Greyhound Technology

This next example is about a technology company that has been unsuccessful in articulating a clear Y vision.

Like many in its industry, Greyhound Technology was founded by a small team that left a much larger technology company, which the team members felt wasn't innovating fast enough. The Greyhound Technology founders worked in a garage for a year, perfecting their approach. What Greyhound Technology was able to accomplish was an entirely new combination of hardware and software to manage power use and heat dissipation by servers. As data centers grew throughout the 1990s and 2000s, the company had huge success, even managing through the dot-com bubble and global financial crisis. However, the storm that ultimately threatened the company's future came in the form of a cloud, *the cloud* to be specific. The cloud allows companies to store their data in remote servers, often managed by outside companies, and to pay those other companies based on the amount of server capacity they need at any one time, rather than making an up-front capital investment. It has revolutionized both how servers are used and who buys them, hitting Greyhound Technology right where it lives.

Historically, Greyhound Technology sold its offering to the IT directors who managed their company's servers. Now, with so many companies outsourcing their servers via the cloud, Greyhound Technology must sell to a small number of cloud providers, who demand much lower prices in exchange for volume. These companies are competing at extremely low margins as they build share, so they are sensitive to every small cost. Over time, competitors have mimicked Greyhound Technology's products. While they do not offer the same performance quality, they are close enough to be considered low-cost substitutes.

The arrival of cloud computing occurred over several years. Yet the leadership at Greyhound Technology has not been able to clearly define its go-forward strategy. The strong engineering culture at Greyhound Technology creates a belief that market challenges can all be solved through product innovation. In fact, Greyhound Technology has released a series of new products that run private clouds (where companies build their own server farms) or hybrid clouds (where companies use a combination of public and private clouds). However, the shift to the public cloud seems unstoppable (at least at this moment), and revenues are falling. Some analysts are calling for Greyhound Technology to be acquired by another company or to acquire a more innovative company itself.

The CEO of Greyhound Technology is one of the original founders of the company, and like many founders, he finds it hard to imagine that large change is necessary. His Y strategy is a minor variation of the X strategy. If there are times when a Y vision can be too aggressive, there are also times when a Y strategy can be too timid. Here we have an example of a company that is struggling with the definition of XY, not because Y is too far from X, but because Y is too close to X. As a result, the sales enablement team struggles to create meaningful messaging and approaches for the salespeople. From the salespeople's perspective, it seems like they are expected to offer their customers five different flavors of vanilla. New terms, new processes, even new offerings, but the same vision. Ultimately, the strategy is not inspiring employees, or Wall Street analysts, for that matter. As often happens in these cases, some leaders and top sellers are leaving Greyhound Technology for more innovative competitors or going to other tech firms.

Let's turn now to an example of how to successfully change the way people sell.

Fischer Bank

Fischer is a global bank, based in Europe. It has four primary divisions: a consumer bank, a wealth management division, an investment bank, and a corporate bank. Built up from acquisitions over two decades, the bank has struggled to operate as a single entity. When a new CEO was appointed several years ago, he made it his top priority to improve the bank's cross-selling effectiveness.

Because the bank was built on so many acquisitions, there were separate cultures and operating strategies in different units (and even within each unit). More critical was that people in each unit did not have relationships with people in the other units, so they did not trust them. The new CEO, whom we'll call Oskar Becker, set out to change how these groups operated. He focused on three divisions: the wealth management business, the investment bank, and the corporate banking division.

It was quite typical at the time for a wealth management advisor to have a client who was also the CFO of a publicly held company. However, historically there was little or no chance that the advisor would refer that CFO to Fischer's investment bank or corporate bank, even though the CFO is the ideal customer for those units. These advisors were reluctant to make referrals because they feared that something would go wrong with the work done by the other units that would threaten the wealth management relationship. The same situation was equally true for the other units. Both the investment banking and corporate banking units had executive-level clients who were perfect prospects for the wealth management group, but they would not provide referrals for the same reason. All that everyone saw was downside risk.

Becker decided that the bank needed to begin operating with a cross-selling mindset. To that end, he launched a program that took the top 1,000 bankers worldwide through a simulation where they were confronted by clients who had needs that could be served by all three units, though they were currently working with only one division. The banker with the existing relationship had to figure out, by collaborating with people in other units, how to cross-sell this client. Equally important, the bankers had to preserve and expand their current business.

The competitive simulation required teams composed of people across units to create a plan for cross-selling this client. Then they had to present to the client across a series of meetings. The clients were played by top executives at Fischer Bank, which increased the pressure. The program also included a workshop where bankers described their top customers and formed plans to work together to cross-sell them. After the program, those plans were put into action and tracked.

Taking people through the process of planning and selling together had several outcomes. First, just the process of working together in a high-stakes competitive situation built trust. That made it easier for people to work together after the program. Second, the bankers began to see that cross-selling could work, and they were learning and practicing the language and conversations that could be effective. Third, they could see that top management took this effort very seriously. The most important outcome, however, was the financial results. Within a year of the program, Fischer Bank identified $1 billion in net new assets attributable to cross-selling directly driven by the program.

In this example, the Y vision was a different way of selling. It involved selling with colleagues in other divisions to offer clients a wider range of products and services. (The X approach was continuing to sell in silos.) What made the effort successful was that the XY approach was clear: continuing to sell independently while also finding opportunities to cross-sell collaboratively. What made the effort successful quickly was that Fischer Bank took its top people through a simulation of XY. That enabled people to picture and to feel what they needed to do.

Exactitude

Now let's look at an example of a company that successfully changed what it sold and did so by identifying the XY midpoint clearly.

Exactitude was the first company to put business tax software into the cloud. As an alternative to expensive in-house software systems, Exactitude had fast success, experiencing exponential growth for a decade, while legacy players in its industry took time to adapt their products for cloud-based use. Over time though, competitive offerings emerged. Exactitude has held onto its market dominance by offering a faster, simpler product.

The visionary leader of Exactitude began articulating the future for the company a few years ago. That future involves offering more cloud-based software to help businesses more quickly and more simply address a range of business functions. This is the Y future for Exactitude, providing its customers with a range of cloud-based business software better than they can obtain elsewhere.

Exactitude has launched products that are complementary to its original business tax offering. It now has a set of cloud-based software offerings that replace the need for expensive payroll services, and it is launching a performance management system to make it easier to provide employees with fast feedback using mobile devices.

Sellers at Exactitude are segmented by the size of the company they sell to: small business, medium business, or large companies. Salespeople in all three segments offer the full range of Exactitude's offerings, since the buyers they work with are often responsible for investments across tax, payroll, and human resources.

The introduction of the new product offerings to the original business tax software is an example of how the XY approach can work successfully. Most customers enter through the X door, and all Exactitude salespeople can tell the X story. Then they have a clear process for upselling the customer to Y. While the leaders at Exactitude would be the first to say that they have made mistakes, are still learning, and expect even better results in the future, they would be proud to share their success to date.

For Exactitude, the Y vision was to have a range of cloud-based software that simplifies their customers' business needs, particularly in niches underserved by the big software providers or better served through cloud-based offerings. In launching this vision, Exactitude leaders have been careful to frame it within the existing approach to selling business tax software. That helps create the XY clarity that salespeople need. For example, Exactitude carefully communicates the new conversation that sellers should have with existing buyers. That conversation includes discussion about the existing X product (business tax software) and the new Y products (payroll and performance management software).

When some companies expand their brand, they often frame it in entirely new terms, trying to become a very different company. Exactitude has been careful to frame its new vision as very connected to the core of who the company has always been and what customers have come to expect from it.

Conclusion—Expansive Vision, Incremental Strategy

These examples illustrate several important points about sales transformation. First, as in the Bridgewater example, a transformation can be abandoned if the expectations require moving too fast, without enough time in the XY phase. Second, as in the Greyhound story, the Y vision has to be compelling, not just incremental. Just as the Bridgewater example shows the consequences of moving too quickly, the Greyhound example illustrates being too tentative. In the third example, about Fischer Bank, we begin to see how a clear XY approach can be communicated and to understand the benefits of practicing not just Y but XY. Finally, in the Exactitude story, we see the benefit of an expansive vision with an incremental execution strategy that was easy for salespeople to understand and implement.

CHAPTER 4

Selling in an XY World

S ales transformation is often traumatic for salespeople. It triggers a multiyear process where everything will potentially change. Even if you are a great salesperson, you can't help but have a version of this conversation with yourself and, more often than not, with others:

> I've done too well the past few years for them to mess with me . . . I doubt much will change. Maybe I'll be promoted to global accounts? That would be awesome . . . but the new sales leader doesn't really know me . . . what if I'm demoted to SMB. This is crazy . . . I've got to focus on this proposal . . . it's due Friday.
>
> Even if I do stay in my current job, will they change my customer list? Why am I killing myself to do a proposal for a customer that I probably won't even keep? Because I'm a good rep and they'll take care of me even if I don't keep the account. Got to focus! Who am I kidding? They'll probably blow up the comp plan anyway.

What if the comp plan does change? This isn't what I signed up for . . . I'm making myself crazy over things that will never happen . . . Breathe . . . What if they give my favorite customer to Steven? He'll destroy all my work of the past three years . . . What if I get some of Steven's accounts? That will be worse than starting from zero . . . I could be Steven's boss in the new world . . . I'd finally do what everyone knows needs to be done with him . . . Wait, Steven knows our new leader from their former employer . . . what if he becomes my boss? Oh well . . . I know one thing for sure . . . I'm not doing this proposal right now . . . I'm exhausted.

Every few months, new announcements are made, and the blank space in between is filled with countless versions of the best- and worst-case scenarios. The instant messages and lunch conversations are filled with rumors about what will happen next. One of the unfortunate aspects of big change initiatives is the way they prime people to go into wait-and-see mode. As a result, the human mind obsessively plays out every possible scenario, while discretionary effort disappears and sales productivity is destroyed.

One of the beautiful advantages of seeing change through an X → XY → Y lens (as opposed to an X → Y lens) is that much of the ambiguity and weariness described above can be reduced. There is simply less shock. Shock drives our systems to shut down to preserve vital functions. It is not a condition that encourages adaptive behaviors, so we want to avoid shock. Yet by organizing corporate initiatives around big announcements and town hall meetings where we celebrate Y and begin to minimize X, we unintentionally create some lesser version of shock, one where people withdraw and hesitate.

Imagine it differently. What if the big announcement is not all about Y but instead it's about Y and XY? Here's an example: It's easy to think that Steve Jobs's famous iPod launch was all about Y (the iPod), but in reality it was also about X (the CD). Check it out on YouTube; it's fun to watch because it has nowhere near the production quality of later Apple launches. Most of the presentation is devoted to explaining XY: how CD content can be imported onto the iPod. That's the model that sales leaders have to follow in announcing a sales transformation. Not the black turtleneck and high-waist jeans, but combining the elation around the new Y with fairly pragmatic discussion of the XY integration process.

Too often today, salespeople are left to navigate the XY phase on their own. They rely on experimentation, their peers, and social media to figure out what to do. Yes, it sounds like a story of kids learning about sex or drugs in the back of the bus. Don't let this happen to your team!

The good news is that there is a lot the salesperson can do on his or her own to shift from selling only X to selling XY, with or without good leadership. Earlier in this book, we mentioned that the X-to-Y transformation could apply to selling something new or to selling in a new way. For the purposes of this chapter and those that immediately follow, we are going to focus on selling something new.

Network Adapter

There are times where selling Y requires finding new customers, but the much more common situation is selling Y to existing customers, or more accurately beginning to include Y in what you already sell to your customers, to make the XY combination solution.

Now while the customer company may be the same as before, the individual decision-making buyers often change. Typically in an X-to-Y sales transformation, salespeople need to shift from selling to buyers who *are responsible for single functions and implementation activities* to selling to executives who *oversee multiple functions, create strategies, and set budgets.*

We think the notion of "economic buyers," "technical buyers," and "users" is outdated. The idea of buyers with distinct, siloed interests comes from a time when there were more layers of middle management in companies than there are today. Buyers today know they have to take economic, technical, and user considerations into account simultaneously.

It takes considerable time to add executive buyers to your existing network. While there are lots of ideas and even complete books about how to access executives, our research shows that only a few techniques work consistently.

- **Internal referrals.** Getting your existing buyers to introduce you to the executive is often the best path. You then enter the executive's office with credibility. Obtaining this internal referral requires you to get smarter and smarter about your customer's business, asking questions about strategy and operations that your existing contacts can't answer, until finally they refer you to someone who can. When they do, bringing them along and making them look smart is key to making this approach work and to cementing your long-term relationship with them.

- **External referrals.** The other way to have immediate credibility is to be referred by someone the executive trusts from outside the executive's organization. Fortunately, in today's LinkedIn world, this is markedly easier than it was a decade or more ago. The idea here is to find a connection between the executive you want to see and someone in your network who would be willing to make the referral on your behalf.

- **Warm calls.** The last approach that works is a not-quite-cold approach. Here you identify a top strategic priority for the executive, and in very few words (less than three short sentences) you explain how your XY combination can help that executive achieve that priority more quickly, at a higher quality, less expensively, or with less risk. Any one of those will do. That e-mail will often get the meeting.

You will also likely need to expand your network beyond executives. There will be stakeholders and subject-matter experts for Y that are different than those for X. In selling XY, you'll need to deal with the stakeholders and subject-matter experts for both X and Y.

Making the Case for XY

One key to building this expanded network is to have your messaging clear. People will think of your company as an X company. They may already be aware of competitors whom they think of as Y companies. You will need a fast, simple explanation of why your company's ability to do X and Y together as XY is an advantage to them. Remember, if you're an incumbent supplier, they already trust you, so take advantage of that. If they've already been intrigued by Y as a result of approaches from other companies, position your offering as a way to start experimenting with Y but in an XY manner that contains less risk.

The new messaging will need to occur on several levels. The first is the new way you describe your offering, which we just covered. But there is also a need to explain your company's new strategy. Customers need to be assured that the Y offering is a long-term strategic investment for your organization and not just a set of quick-fix add-on features meant to stave off the competition.

Having both these conversations—the offering conversation and the strategy conversation—can be made easier by having others with you. In the first situation, where you are discussing your company's new XY offering, it can be helpful to have an expert in Y with you. This can be a solutions engineer, a product expert, or even a vertical industry expert who can speak to what your customer's competitors are doing. Many companies create "consultants" who specialize in Y or in helping customers make the transition to Y. And let's face it: often the Y business is acquired, rather than innovated. Frequently this second person comes from the acquired company. It's your job to make sure that person accompanying you can speak to XY and not just advocate Y, which will confuse your messaging. You, too, need to be able to speak effectively to XY; you can't just rely on the specialist to convey the message.

For the second situation, where you are describing your company's strategy, it is often best to have your sales manager or even a more senior company leader be involved. That adds credibility about your company's commitment to this new strategy. It is also another method of getting access to an executive since you can pursue a like-title meeting.

It isn't only your external network that will need to change. Your internal network will have to be adapted too. All those Y experts we mentioned earlier will become critical to your success. If pricing or payment systems are changing, you'll want new connections in those departments. You will probably need different resources to help you with contracting, implementation, and customer service issues.

Competitive Positioning

Let's assume your customer buys X from you today. There are three typical competitive situations:

Situation A
Your customer buys X from others, as well as you, but does not yet buy Y from anyone

Situation A is the most advantageous to you. You can be the hero who introduces your customer to Y, and you can do it in a way that is low risk to your customer (by selling an XY combo). In making this introduction, you want to ensure that you do not take advantage of your customer's inexperience in any way. If you do, you'll leave yourself wide open to an entry by a smart competitor.

You also do not want to wait too long to introduce Y. It's easy to mislead yourself into thinking that a customer organization isn't ready for Y or isn't aware of Y. You'll know that you've been too polite when suddenly you discover that your customer just completed a giant deal with a Y competitor that you knew nothing about, in part because your customer didn't know that you even offered Y. More and more customers are expecting the salespeople who call on them to bring new ideas and test existing assumptions. We will explore best practices around how, when, and with whom to have these conversations in Part 3.

Situation B
Your customer has begun to buy Y from a competitor while still buying X from you

As we mentioned in "Making the Case for XY," above, there are good reasons a company should feel more comfortable buying Y from you than from a competitor it hasn't worked with before. Often those new Y competitors are smaller organizations without strong track records or references. So the company should buy from you, but it is already buying from your competitor.

Often it is a separate small buying center that first innovates with a Y supplier. It may not even be someone you've talked to. But you now need to ensure that the Y supplier doesn't use that as a toehold into the larger organization. This is your time to present a compelling case for how your company can take care of the customer's Y needs and how you can do it with lower risk than a pure-Y company can.

While your competitor is looking for small niche buyers to bite off, you need to pursue an enterprisewide strategy. Just like in politics, all good strategies start with shoring up your base. You've got to create unique XY value by starting with those who already know and like you. Their continued advocacy for your incumbent position is vital.

Situation C
Your customer has begun to buy XY from a competitor while still buying X from you

This is the most dangerous situation.

We write in this book primarily about X → XY → Y as a sales transformation model, but it is also a more general change management model. As we noted in Chapter 1, sales is change management. So you can apply the X → XY → Y to your customer situation too. (We will go deeply into this concept in Part 3.) In our view, owning the XY state is where the power is. It is where the biggest challenges lie, to be sure, but it is also where the most value is created. So if a competitor has already laid claim to the XY space, you will have more difficulty defending your position. You are left with three primary alternatives:

1. **Defend your existing X business.** This is a necessary approach though not a winning long-term strategy on its own. You can expect to see large downward pressure on prices for X over time.

2. **Attack the competitor in the XY space.** This strategy works best if you have a genuinely differentiated value proposition than the competitor who is already offering XY. Often, however, what suppliers like to think of as

genuinely differentiated is not. The other strategy here is one of locking in buying centers. Make a big effort to sell XY to your most loyal buyers. Splitting the account is better than losing the account.

3. **Jump to selling pure Y**. In this approach, you move quickly to positioning your company as a much better Y provider than the company that is currently offering the buyer XY. You, essentially, are leapfrogging your competitor. To make this strategy work, you need to leverage the best Y people in your organization and act as if you were a company that only sold Y. One risk with this approach is that you are inviting your customer to obtain bids from other true pure-Y providers.

Whichever path you choose, remember that your customer is in a transformation too. Act as if you have a fiduciary responsibility to guide the customer through that change process. You can never go wrong by doing the right thing for the customer.

Selling X in an XY World

Many salespeople find themselves selling X in an XY world. This can happen for several reasons:

- Your company has not yet created a Y or XY offering, but competitors have.

- Your company is moving to XY, but you are not assigned to the first adoption wave.

- You just don't get XY and aren't ready to make the move.

So you're left selling X for now. There are important ways in which the selling of X changes in an XY world, even if you as an individual are not yet selling XY or Y.

The presence of Y changes the way customers think about buying X. That means you need to recognize that you are positioning your offering not only against other X competitors but also against Y and possibly XY. It is also likely that your buyers may begin to bring other stakeholders to the table. While it is sometimes a natural first reaction to dismiss those additional people, you'll be much better served by getting to know them and their priorities.

The existence of Y also tends to extend buying cycles, which in turn lengthens sales cycles. More decision makers, more influencers, and more options all drive more complicated and longer decision processes. We'll discuss specific tips for dealing with these complications and delays in Chapters 8 and 9.

Mindset becomes critically important when you are selling X in an XY world. To have fun and to be successful, you have to believe in the continuing value of X. Here are some tips for doing that:

- Decide that you will be the best X seller in the business.

- Recognize that for a long time there will continue to be a large group of customers that want to buy X, not Y. You are the vehicle to help them to do just that.

- Be able to articulate the situations in which a pure-X solution is a better option for customers.

- Don't be afraid of or resist Y. Develop your knowledge about Y. Don't talk trash about Y either; someday you will likely be selling Y—and your customers will be buying Y from someone else if not from you.

As we explain in the later chapter on sales leadership, part of change management is taking good care of the X sellers, even as the XY shift has begun, since not everyone will make the shift at the same time. For sales leaders, that means providing real support to X sellers and recognition of their successes. There's a parallel truth for salespeople whose customers are buying X in an emerging XY world. Those customers need support and recognition too.

Managing the Pipeline

The shift to an XY world dramatically changes the shape and velocity of sales pipelines. As we have mentioned, XY sales cycles are usually longer. That means you have to have the right mix of X and XY opportunities in your funnel to achieve your targets. You can't go all XY in the beginning; you need to continue selling X. You also need to build a sufficient volume of XY opportunities to compensate for the increased sales cycle time.

Ultimately, you'll change your priorities again as you move from selling XY to selling mostly Y, but the steps will be quite similar: watch the mix, continue selling some XY, and build the Y funnel volume.

Conclusion—Managing the Business

When you're only selling X, you have one business to manage. But once you start selling XY, you really have three businesses to manage: the X business, the XY business, and the Y business. Each of those businesses (by which we mean the corresponding sets of opportunities, customers, and revenue) requires different thinking. So life gets more complicated quickly. But a more complicated life is preferable to an unemployed life or even an employed life characterized by decline and underperformance.

If you are a salesperson, you'll want to see how customers are changing their buying routines, in Part 2, and how salespeople can excel by helping their customers get through their own X-to-Y transformations, in Part 3. In Part 2 we also discuss the causes for the buying delays that are happening so frequently now, and in Part 3 we explain what to do about them.

If you are a salesperson who aspires to management and leadership roles, then this whole book is for you.

CHAPTER 5

Sales Management in an XY World

S ales managers are generally faced with an impossible job. As we'll explore later in this book, they are expected to do far too much in the time they have available. That impossible job is made even harder during periods of major change, as when a sales transformation is announced. Now they are expected to communicate with confidence about a new set of priorities that they themselves don't fully understand or accept.

It is moments like these that test the sales manager. Most sales managers got their jobs because they were so great at selling X that their companies promoted them hoping to duplicate their success. At the time when they need confidence the most, waves of insecurity and self-doubt can make sales managers begin to question their own judgment. Let's look at what often happens by seeing a sales transformation from the perspective of three sales managers who have been brought together by their sales leader, Sarah, to discuss some major changes.

Carlos was brought in a few years ago from another company that exclusively sold Y. That company had a "let's move fast and break things" culture. While he generally has a collaborative nature, Carlos is intent on reestablishing his new company as the market leader by helping it sell a lot more Y. Because he has had great personal success selling Y and because he is more familiar than his colleagues with the Y market, he wants everyone to be selling Y as quickly as possible.

Andre seems to have given up before the sales transformation process has even started. No one on his team, including himself, has been able to make a Y sale. If Y is the future, Andre is beginning to see himself as the past. He's wondering if there are openings at a competitor he knows who is still committed to selling X.

Claire has a top salesperson on her team who successfully sold Y recently, but now there are major implementation issues that are consuming a lot of time for both Claire and her salesperson. As a result, Claire finds herself questioning whether the company is really ready to sell Y. She is skeptical about how fast the company can move to selling Y, and she is ready to challenge Sarah's plans.

Whereas they once saw themselves as top performers being promoted to the next level of responsibility, sales managers can now begin to see themselves as corporate middlemen for the first time. Their dream of leading their team to unparalleled success is now tempered by a recognition that they are operating under significant constraints. At this point many sales managers realize they have been given this job to execute, not to lead. They are cascading strategies from above, carrying out orders from above, conducting activities designated by others, and calculating metrics and reports for others. This situation is rarely permanent, though, and once the new definition of "great" is accepted, the sales managers can focus on leading again.

As managers are dealing with their own demons, their teams are looking to them for guidance. Most salespeople genuinely want to learn and improve. They want feedback and direction. They seek clarity from their sales manager about how they will be measured. Salespeople also need help navigating their way around their own companies and handling tricky customer situations. However, what often happens is that the sales manager is not able to provide the needed assistance on any kind of consistent basis. There simply isn't time. Even though managers are being pressured to "spend more time coaching," they are also being asked to administer more reports, validate the CRM outputs, update the forecast, and work on next year's budget. At the same time, they have to fill two open spots on their team, work with HR to terminate an underperformer, and mediate a battle between one of their reps and the pricing department.

Then they are asked to launch a change initiative in the midst of all this. Fortunately, there is a group of sales managers who see these times of change as the answer rather than the problem. They use the sales transformation to restructure things to make their lives, and those of their team, easier. They use new strategies to give people hope and a more meaningful sense of the future. But most sales managers don't fall into that category.

Instead they don't quite break down, but they shift into low gear. They see a rough road ahead and they downshift. They push their teams a little less hard because they are less sure of what matters. They express more cynicism because they are confused and don't see a clear path forward. They begin to describe decisions as "political" and as being determined by who has power now, rather than by what is best for the company, its people, and its customers. They begin to disengage at the exact moment their sales leaders need them to be more active than ever.

Big shifts exacerbate these reactions. So when companies announce an X-to-Y transformation, the response can be problematic due to the scale of the change. The direct X → Y approach creates a picture of success (Y) that most sales managers can't see. They can't identify someone on their teams who is doing it well. They don't know what great Y selling looks like, and if they can't picture it, they can't believe in it, let alone explain it to others.

Let's look at why the X → XY → Y approach works better. Leaders still have to articulate their vision of a Y business. But Y does not become the short-term picture of success. Instead, XY does. That means they can communicate to sales managers a picture of how X and Y will be sold at the same time, often to the same customers. It implies a recognition that the skills required to sell X successfully (which sales managers have been emphasizing with their teams until now) have value in the new strategy. Most important, the X → XY → Y approach requires a smaller incremental change than a full direct-to-Y strategy, so it's more digestible.

Embedded in the X → XY → Y approach is the need to measure X, XY, and Y, not just Y. For sales managers, that means the metrics do not change as dramatically or as quickly as in an X → Y transformation.

The lives of sales managers during sales transformations can certainly be made easier by sales leaders doing the right things, and we'll look more at that in the next chapter. But for now, let's focus on what sales managers can do themselves.

The Winning Mindset

There is one main differentiator that shapes a sales manager's experience during a sales transformation. It determines whether the manager resists the change or adopts it, whether the manager is seen by his team as an authentic leader or a simple messenger, and whether the manager sees his future at this company or another. That differentiator is *mindset*.

Mindset is the missing ingredient in many failed execution efforts, according to research by the company we are part of, BTS, on what drives successful execution. Mindset means individual belief in the strategy, belief that it is the right strategy for the company, for our customers, for our employees, and for me. People who have adopted the winning mindset feel the urgency to begin implementing the strategy immediately.

For sales managers in a sales transformation, the first step involves making it a personal priority to fully understand the strategy. It is the sales manager's obligation to ensure he understands the strategy. It's easy to blame leaders for not communicating the strategy correctly or fully, but no strategy is communicated perfectly. The managers must take this on themselves. They have to ask good questions, read everything they can, and talk about it with others, without cynicism.

There are a number of specific tips that make it easier to adopt and maintain the right mindset. First, recognize that the X → XY → Y journey is a long one. In our experience it lasts a minimum of three years and sometimes as long as a decade. Plus, remember that it doesn't end at Y. As we said in Chapter 2, it really looks like X → XY → Y → YZ → Z, etc. We have entered a world of continuous sales transformation. The sales managers who recognize that and become comfortable with it will become the next generation of sales leaders.

Second, on that long journey, it works better not to become attached to just one possible outcome. Recognize that there are multiple ways of achieving results, multiple paths to success. Be clear about the strategy, be committed to the vision, but be flexible about the execution. Celebrate the big milestones, but don't let the implementation obscure the achievement of measurable progress toward the goal. Measure how much progress was achieved toward the vision (e.g., six new XY customers this month) rather than whether a specific step in the project plan was accomplished on time.

A third way to ensure the right mindset is to recognize that as a sales manager, your most important role may well be as the "chief priority officer" for your team. That is, people look to you to establish what should be important to them, how they should spend their time, and what accounts and opportunities they should pursue. By fully accepting this role and by doing the hard work required to make informed decisions, you can have a giant impact on your team's results. One of the first things you'll want to do is to challenge the status quo. Question whether current sales activities are really driving results. So often they do not. Figure out what activities should be priorities in the XY environment.

Here are some tips that will help you in establishing the correct prioritization structure:

- **Use data to inform your point of view.** Today's corporate environments are filled with data. Leverage that data to better understand what is happening. (Where is your pipeline strong or weak? What patterns can you see in sales cycle length?) Focus not only on individual performance but on what is happening more broadly in the business.

- **Evolve your point of view based on conversations with people you trust.** Make sure you're talking frequently to peers in similar positions and to people in very different roles. Get exposed to alternative thinking. See contrary viewpoints as ideas worth exploring rather than just the positions of other camps.

- **Seek perspective from people outside your company, particularly customers.** Warren Buffett has said that when your business is in trouble, the first people to talk to are your customers. They will tell you what you should do. Prospects are another crucial audience. Sometimes the potential customers you are not currently winning are those with the most important message for what your future needs to be.

- **Be open to changing direction quickly when you get strong evidence that it is necessary.** Rather than big changes, though, try to deploy fast experiments that deliver data for better longer-term decisions.

In any case, managers who fail often do so because they try to control too many things. Staying focused on a few things that really matter will make it easier for you and for your team. Set the top priorities, communicate them frequently, and measure progress against them. Keeping it that simple will ensure that not only you maintain the right mindset but your team does as well.

How to Guide Your Team

Leading your team is different in an XY environment. You have to show that you value X, XY, and Y, not just Y, and not just X as you have in the past. That may mean that a different kind of sales management is needed. And the right sales manager for an XY environment might not be the same as the perfect one for a pure-Y environment (though we know that Z, and more change, is coming).

So how do you make XY sales management work? It's mostly about communicating a vision and a flexible plan to achieve the vision. Many sales managers fail to establish a vision for their team because they feel their company vision will suffice. But the company vision does not get salespeople excited every day. Every sales team needs a vision that describes its unique picture of success. It's the sales manager's job to come up with that vision.

In this case, your vision may be mostly about Y, but your plan will incorporate milestone goals for X, for XY, and for Y. You acknowledge to your team that while we're committing to the vision of Y, it is unrealistic to ever have the execution plan more than 80 percent right initially. You will have to make adjustments along the way.

Those adjustments may take the form of experiments. You may ask your team to try out some specific XY selling techniques with a small group of clients and then evaluate how the techniques worked. Or you might invite a Y specialist to attend upcoming account review sessions to see if the specialist can add ideas on how to introduce Y to more X accounts. The key here is to make a big distinction between decisions that have been reached around the sales process and approach ("This is the way we all work now") and experiments that will inform the process in the future ("Let's try this and see what happens"). Salespeople can manage very little ambiguity, so keep the settled decisions and potential experiments distinctly separate.

As you and your team move through the X → XY → Y journey, you will encounter all sorts of compensation issues. Don't become alarmed. One of the most common change-resistance techniques that sales managers use to forestall sales transformations is to say that nothing can change until the comp plan changes. While it is true that salespeople's behavior is affected by how they're compensated, it's not true that you can't begin changing behavior until the comp plan is fixed. If that were true, nothing would ever change because the comp plan always lags strategy. By their nature, comp plans can only be changed once a year, and there can be significant negative unintended impacts from making too great a change at any one time. The compensation system will always be behind. And that, of course, just makes the sales manager's job harder.

The best guiding principle when changing incentive systems is that you have to ensure that no one will get unfairly rich or go unfairly hungry with the new plan. That will build trust.

Conclusion—Retaining Your People

Of course you want to retain your best people, and probably even your average performers, since replacing them is time consuming and expensive. But here is the problem: your team can't believe in something you don't. By setting clear priorities and focusing on your own mindset, you will inspire trust and enable the members of your team to see success paths for themselves. By setting attainable near-term goals and rewarding success, you'll increase confidence and accelerate their development. They'll then be able to manage the changing mix of business in their pipelines, and you will ensure that your people don't lose out and leave.

If you are a sales manager or are aspiring to sales leadership roles, you will be particularly interested in Part 4 of this book. It is where we go into detail on the three ways that sales managers can drive an XY sales transformation (by leading people, developing people, and executing their plan) and where we show what great sales leadership looks like in an XY world. Of course, everything before Part 4 sets the groundwork for those ideas, by analyzing how customers see and create change and by exploring how to help customers as they go through their own X-to-Y transformations.

CHAPTER 6

Sales Leadership in an XY World

In our experience, most sales transformations are driven by sales leaders who are new to their roles. Some are driven by new CEOs in collaboration with existing sales leaders. But it's rare that executives wake up and decide to make major changes to the businesses they have been running.

Sales transformations are almost always triggered by one or more of four developments:

- Consistently flat or declining revenues

- Activity from competitors (especially new entrants) that threatens the future of the existing revenue base

- The approaching obsolescence of a key product or the introduction of a radically new product

- Quickly changing customer expectations

Typically, when these developments start to occur, a new sales leader is put into place, often from outside the company. That is the first indication that a big change is coming.

If you have been with your company for a long time, you probably helped to build the X business. You may, then, not be very comfortable with the Y business. You likely even question whether it's the right business to pursue and find yourself saying things like "We should stick with our core competencies." But if you do want to get on board, you might find someone to pair up with. Look either for an internal Y advocate or even for an external partner to help you get started.

Great sales leaders can see the marketplace change and the early signs that X is on the decline and Y is on the rise. They begin to consider questions about whether it is best to create a separate Y sales force and whether the existing X sales force is capable of selling Y. They have to resolve hard questions about the speed of the change and be ready to answer questions from the board like, "How do we continue to justify selling X when we know the future is Y?"

Let's look at the situation that Sarah, the leader of the three sales managers described in the previous chapter—Carlos, Andre, and Claire—must now confront:

> The time for closed-door executive meetings is over. Although she is sure that things will come up that she hasn't thought of, Sarah is confident that she has done all she can to develop the sales transformation strategy that will lead to success.
>
> She has been authentic and as transparent as possible with her team; however, Sarah is also careful not

to create unnecessary stress around pending decisions. From her own experiences as a seller and as a sales manager, she knows how paralyzing uncertainty can be, so she has acted fast. She realizes that she has been on a long journey with the executive team, preparing to make the transition from X to Y. The others on her team will need to struggle with many of the same questions the executive team felt it had now answered. Last, she knows this needs to be a conversation, so she is going to bring everyone together for a discussion.

Sarah has decided to host a dinner for her team the evening before the meeting, a decision she will quickly regret. Because she, Andre, and Claire have all been salespeople together, Sarah assumes that a social gathering would be the best way to reassure her team that the executives have been thinking about the right things and value the team members as individuals. However, even before the paper napkin under the calamari grows transparent from the oil, it becomes clear that a deep divide has formed between Carlos and her old friends.

Because he lacks the information that she will share the following day, Carlos's assumptions are wrong, and Sarah spends a fair amount of energy trying to figure out how she can reset him without disengaging him.

And then there are Claire and Andre. Although they both put on their best faces, Claire is clearly angry, and Andre just seems sad. Sarah is caught completely off guard by Andre's attitude.

Claire peppers Sarah with difficult questions throughout the meal. While Sarah appreciates Claire's focus on employee and customer satisfaction, by the time the coffees hit the table, she feels like her parole has come through.

The way to approach these situations is to recognize that change is a journey. You simply can't get everyone selling Y tomorrow. Even if you fired your entire sales force, you likely couldn't find enough experienced Y sellers to replace everyone. Plus, in all likelihood, you have a giant base of revenue with X customers. While conceivably you could sell that business, those X customers will someday be your Y customers. You need those relationships, and you will need those customers to see you as the brand that guided them through their own journey in moving from buying X to buying Y. You don't want to become the boyfriend that dumped them for someone more exciting and then tried to win them back.

In the earliest stages, while you will, intentionally or not, have a small group exclusively selling Y, keeping separate X and Y sales forces beyond that point is a bad idea. Why? Because you need the Y selling behaviors to bleed into the X sales force. You actually want to integrate X and Y sales activities as quickly as possible. That accelerated integration is really at the heart of what we're writing about. In the traditional X → Y way of thinking, it might make sense to watch Y grow and X shrink (though what typically happens is that Y doesn't grow fast enough and X shrinks faster than expected). But the X → XY → Y approach is all about integration, which simplifies messaging, reduces change resistance, limits risk, and makes transformation more manageable.

In the X → XY→ Y model, the most important contribution the sales leader can make is not, surprisingly, articulating the Y vision. It is explaining what XY looks like. There are three simple forms XY typically takes:

1. Salespeople selling an XY combination to a customer

2. Salespeople selling both X and Y to the same customer, but as separate purchases, often to different buyers in the same company

3. Salespeople selling both X and Y but to different customers, selling X to some and Y to others.

Any of these three models work, though the first is the most efficient. However, we typically don't get to choose which model to pursue. It depends on the extent to which the customers are the same for X and Y and the extent to which the decision makers within those customers are the same for X and Y. One thing a sales leader can do is make sure sufficient research has been done to answer those questions before an XY strategy is announced.

Avoiding the Common Error: Choosing the Wrong Destination

Some readers are probably saying, "Great. This is how I've always worked," and what they mean by that is that they have always been incremental and focused on XY. Their mistake is that they are creating a vision for XY without a clear vision for Y. The X → XY → Y approach only works if it is a defined journey over time to Y, with a well-articulated vision for Y and a clear statement of why the future of the business must be Y. Without that emphasis on the ultimate Y destination, without that compelling purpose, people will not be motivated to change behavior. There will be no burning platform, no urgency.

Let's be even clearer: X → XY alone is not a path to sales transformation. It is a path to confusion. In practice, it's even worse than it seems. Typically, leaders who believe in XY do not communicate a vision for XY. What they do is allow XY to germinate, often organically. But at the same time, throughout their organization, there are also other combinations sprouting. Let's call them XA, XB, XC, etc. Without the up-front work to define the desirable and necessary Y future, these sales forces wind up with different teams going different directions. Innovative individuals experiment on their own with whatever combinations they can create to address the changes they see in the marketplace. Salespeople are left confused and often demoralized. This proliferation of alternatives is what creates the flavor-of-the-month mindset that has taught salespeople to ignore change initiatives. Salespeople in this situation report back on employee engagement surveys that they can't see the company's future direction. They start paying attention to job opportunities at companies with better-articulated futures.

Having said that, we are big believers in experimentation, and we'll make recommendations later in the book about beneficial approaches to experimentation. However, experimentation is what you apply to tactics. You shouldn't experiment with multiple visions. The vision work to define Y is difficult and takes time. It requires collecting new data about the changing market, involving the right stakeholders to help analyze it, coming up with alternative scenarios for the future, and ultimately getting alignment about a chosen direction. All of that must happen before the Y future can be communicated and the X → XY → Y path articulated. In any case, announcing what XY might look like before you've committed to a Y future will not only *not* work; it will likely delay your progress.

When leaders mistakenly choose to focus on an XY destination instead of a Y destination with an XY period in the middle, it is not that they have the wrong intentions. It's simply that they don't have a clear model for how to proceed, understandably want to minimize risk, and find it hard to define a new destination. The good news is that this book provides a clear road map for that journey.

Setting the Tone

Times of change can be times of fear or times of opportunity. If the leader doesn't get this right, no one will. There is a set of, admittedly generic, speaking points that almost any sales leader can adapt to his or her needs:

- We are doing well today, and we must stay ahead and keep our edge. (Strength)

- We must always be innovative and changing. (Agility)

- We have the opportunity to do something great! (Opportunity)

- If we thought of this, so have others, so we must act fast. (Urgency)

- I know where we should go. I want to bring as many with me as I can, but I know some won't make it. (Challenge)

- We can't wait for a perfect plan. We will test things and adjust as we go. (Humility)

Getting the tone right is not just about being relentlessly positive, however. Don't be dismissive of concerns that people express. They may think of something you didn't. Or they're working out in their heads what you've already figured out. Don't label them as naysayers or assume they will not come around. By taking what can be perceived as negativity seriously, you enhance your credibility, and your optimistic outlook becomes more believable.

Leadership Qualities

Leading a sales organization through sales transformation is not easy. No magic new set of leadership attributes is required for sales transformation (phew!), but it's worth a few reminders of the things that are most critical:

- **Be transparent and authentic.** Anything you hide will surface and will cost you credibility with the team. Speak with confidence about what you have figured out, and speak with candor about what still needs to be resolved.

- **Communicate.** More than you think necessary. Whenever you're not speaking, people are filling in the blanks with the worst-possible scenario for themselves. People need to hear the same messages over and over before they adopt them as their own. They need to hear them from you; they need to hear them from executives above you; they need to hear them from their managers; and they need to hear them from their peers.

- **Give people time.** More often than not, a leadership team has been thinking and talking about the changes that need to be made for a very long time. Great leaders recognize that concepts that have become assumptions for the core team will be new to the broader audience. Give people time to get comfortable with these concepts. Continue to return to them and to the thinking that drove your conclusions.

- **Know that you will not get it 100 percent right.** In fact you'll be lucky to get it 80 percent right. Communicating this to the team will cause uncertainty for some, but your best people will respect you more. It is admirable to try new things and make adjustments if they aren't successful. Many times when we guide sales leaders through sales transformations, we encourage them to think about the initiative that they will likely cancel or change early in the transformation. When that takes place, it deserves as much communication as the celebration of a success. People will then believe that you're more invested in making the transformation work than in having been right.

Conclusion—Past and Future

In the XY world, great sales leadership involves demonstrating tremendous respect for the past and clarity about the future. If you're new to the company, you will alienate people if you don't speak with reverence for the company's legacy and past success. That honoring of the past must be met with an equally enthusiastic and reasoned (not just hopeful) articulation of the future. That clear future vision is what will inspire people to expend discretionary effort to be successful.

After looking next at the customers' perspective, we will look at X → XY → Y sales transformations from the perspective of salespeople first, then sales managers, and finally sales leaders.

PART 2

A Change in Buying

CHAPTER 7

How Customers View the X-to-Y Shift

Customers see change differently than salespeople do. It's as if customers are on a moving train and salespeople are on the platform at various stations. Each group has a different sense of what's moving or changing.

Let's look at an example from real life, though the details have been changed to provide anonymity. Phillips Connelly is a global accounting firm. Like most professional service firms, it is highly decentralized and allows the partners to run their businesses fairly independently. However, the company manages its profitability by consolidating many back-office functions, and all offices are required to use those centralized services.

A few years ago, in violation of those rules, the Saõ Paulo office began contracting with a local company to create smartphone apps that its clients could use to make payroll inquiries. One app allowed employees of client companies to see their paystub on their phone as soon as it was issued.

When the members of the centralized application development team inside the IT function at Phillips Connelly found out about this innovation, they immediately brought in the firm's top leadership. Initially the logical response seemed to be to shut down the outsourcing of app development. If the leadership allowed every office to do that, the economies of scale of centralization would vanish. But instead, the CEO decided that not only could São Paulo continue with its approach, but the apps that were created would now be available to the entire firm to use with clients around the world. This announcement created some confusion throughout the company about what other rules might no longer be enforced.

Because the apps were unique, several Phillips Connelly offices outside Brazil adopted them quite quickly. A few offices rejected them entirely. Most offices experimented with the new apps, while continuing to work with the central applications development function and its offerings for clients. In effect, these offices were adopting an XY approach.

That is typically what happens in real life. For customers, change usually occurs organically. One team starts doing something differently, and no one even notices. Then another team learns about it and starts doing the same thing. Before long, many teams are experimenting with the new approach and people begin to notice.

As a result, the adoption curves for customers mimic those for XY selling. As was true for XY selling, people think the distribution curve for customers taking a new approach to something looks like the Stage 2 curve in Figure 7.1.

Figure 7.1   Perception of Stage 2.

But it really looks like the curve in Figure 7.2.

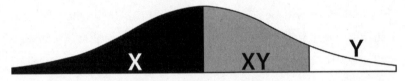

Figure 7.2   Reality of Stage 2.

Why is that important? For one thing, it is critical to sales-people selling into those companies. Let's go back to the Phillips Connelly story. Picture a seller representing a company providing cloud-based storage services and calling on the central application development team within the IT function. The data storage needs of Phillips Connelly are now quite different from when the company was a pure-X (all centralized) firm. That salesperson has to also recognize that the company is still far from being a pure-Y (all decentralized) firm. To sell effectively to Phillips Connelly, the salesperson has to be able to demonstrate an understanding of the nuanced XY world that the firm now operates in, with some applications built centrally and some built locally and then shared globally. Sellers do best when they identify X-to-Y change within their customers' organizations and assist with the XY stage of change, where the most value can be created.

The other kind of change that occurs in customer organizations is top down. The executive team decides on a new strategy or a new way of executing the existing strategy. Let's say that after several quarters of weak earnings, the management of a large bank decides to consolidate five customer service call centers into two. Your immediate response might be to say that there are either five call centers (X) or two call centers (Y); there is no XY in that example. But there is. There will be a period—often a long one—when all five call centers are still operating but three of them know they will shut down. That is the XY period. The dynamics at the three that will close will be quite different from those at the two that will stay open, and some people from the centers that are closing will probably transfer to those that will stay open. These situations inevitably breed ambiguity, in part precisely because leadership makes great efforts to describe what Y will look like but is more opaque about the X-to-Y transition. That leaves people who can be in the XY state for months confused and disoriented.

Now what does this mean to the salespeople? Once again, they become more valuable to the bank if they can help with the X-to-Y transition. Helping means not just knowing what Y looks like but knowing how to get there, and that means understanding the complexities of the XY state and how to manage them.

With all the change occurring in businesses today, the situation we now have is salespeople going through X-to-Y transitions in their own companies selling to customers who are experiencing separate (and multiple) X-to-Y transitions in their organizations. Buyers in the customer organizations are questioning their own judgment, dealing with new stakeholders, and managing through ambiguity, just as leaders and managers are in sales forces undergoing an X-to-Y change. In the next chapters, we'll look deeper into what is happening in customer organizations and then, in Part 3, provide some very concrete advice for salespeople navigating this new world.

CHAPTER 8

Turbulent Skies

Please return to your seats and keep your seat belts fastened.

It has been a long week. You've declared this a no–e-mail flight and are just getting ready to start a movie. Apart from the fact that you prefer the aisle and got the window, the flight has been relatively uneventful. Just as the person next to you is handed her plastic thimble of carbonated sugar water, the plane drops left and then sharply right, lifts a bit, and then settles into steady bumps. The "Fasten Seat Belt" light comes on with a ping, and the woman next to you seems almost as happy as you are that she didn't spill anything on you. Although you've been in this situation many times before, it is still unsettling.

The bumps taper off. Just as you begin to relax, the captain announces, "Flight attendants, please take your seats." The gravel road you've been traveling suddenly turns into a roller coaster. You're not sure how big the last drop was, but your stomach is in your throat. For 15 minutes or longer, everyone stays put.

A similar phenomenon is happening today at many of your customer organizations. The pace of change has become so fast and so bumpy, that people are staying put. They are, essentially, fastened into their seats. That means decisions don't get made. Projects are delayed. Risk avoidance becomes the chief priority, and initial visions of *what would be great* are set aside for *what is now possible.*

Turbulent Buying Behaviors

Always keep your seat belt fastened when seated.

Let's look at what happens in the customer buying process when the pace of change increases to a point that it causes what we are referring to as "turbulence," which is common in customer organizations going through an X-to-Y change process.

Turbulence drives a fear of change. Customers are reluctant to innovate or experiment. The focus is on small, incremental changes that reduce cost. Past strategies are continued, as long as they have had moderate success. Turbulence increases the likelihood that customers will remain with existing providers. The goal is less to maximize success than to minimize failure.

Because they no longer trust their own judgment, buyers are bringing more stakeholders into the decision-making process. Decisions can be postponed multiple times, even if doing so delays the implementation, and especially if the decision involves the assumption of new risk. A recent study by the Center for Creative Leadership looked at wasted time in corporations around the world. Ninety percent of the survey respondents "blamed their wasted time on too many people being involved in the decision-making processes. Some noted that they have to get approval from three people before being able to order supplies as trivial as a box of paper clips." Managers reported that "it was safer for them personally to require their people to seek out multiple approvals."

In a turbulent environment, customers pressure providers to match any element of a competitor's offering that might reduce risk or cost. Procurement departments take over the conversation.

As the customer's organization hits patches of rough air, legitimate shifts in priorities occur. Buyers know that this is going to happen, so there is added stress around unknown opportunity costs. (In the next chapter, we will explore how this development is reshaping the traditional buying cycle.)

The bottom line is this: buyers can't rely on previous experience to anticipate potential outcomes. The situation becomes exponentially worse when Y is not well defined and XY is ambiguous. Without a clear vision of the future, buyers don't feel safe . . . so they play it safe.

Know Your Buyer

So if your customers are tightly strapped into their seats, anticipating the rough air created by change, is there anything you can do? Yes.

Start by knowing your buyer's decision-making focus. Some fascinating recent research by Heidi Grant Halvorson and

E. Tory Higgins shows that there are two main ways that people focus:

- Promotion-focused people seek gain or advancement. For this group, the worst thing is missing an opportunity to do something great. We're going to refer to these people as "gain maximizers."

- Prevention-focused people seek to avoid mistakes. For this group, the worst thing is failing to avoid a loss. We're going to refer to these people as "loss avoiders."

Neither approach is better than the other (though it's natural to feel an affinity for those who match your own approach). The big issue is making sure you have the right conversation with the right type of buyer. You don't want to emphasize risk avoidance with gain maximizers. You want to focus on the vision of what is possible. But you don't want to emphasize that big vision with loss avoiders. Instead, you want to help them navigate to prevent failure.

Of course, many if not most people sit somewhere on the continuum between these two approaches. But thinking about the poles helps ensure that your messaging is correctly targeted. When there are groups of buyers that contain both types of people, you want to make sure that your messaging addresses both kinds of focus (see Table 8.1).

In later chapters, we'll look at 10 ways to respond when customers are facing significant change and their buying process is slowing down, and we'll explain how to adapt your approach to

Different Communication Approaches

Gain Maximizers	Loss Avoiders
• Vision	• Risks
• Big picture	• Details
• What's possible	• What could go wrong
• Why	• How
• Abstract ideas	• Concrete ideas
• Emotions	• Logic

Table 8.1   Alternative Approaches to Communication

the type of focus of your buyer. But for now, let's examine how gain maximizers and loss avoiders respond to times of change.

Managing Buyers During X-to-Y Change

We can say with considerable confidence that during periods of X-to-Y change, gain maximizers will get excited about moving toward Y, and loss avoiders will be concerned about moving away from X. So if you're a salesperson, you need to assess which type of person you're speaking to, so that you can calibrate your messaging.

More generally, during periods of change, gain maximizers focus on the future. They see possibilities, and they tend to underestimate the cost of change and the time required for change. That's what makes them great entrepreneurs. Many other people would never take the risks that extreme gain maximizers take. Gain maximizers calculate that the desirability of Y exceeds the risk of staying with X and the potential costs of moving from X to Y.

On the other hand, loss avoiders respond to change differently. It would be a mistake to assume that loss avoiders fear change. Many are quite comfortable with change and do their best work during times of change. Because they are so sensitive to what could go wrong, they steer the ship through stormy seas. We mentioned earlier that loss avoiders will be concerned about moving away from X, but that's only part of the story. It's not that they grieve X necessarily or that they are inherently opposed to Y. They just want a thoughtful transition, and so they want all scenarios to be considered. Interestingly, it is the loss avoiders who often become the stewards of the XY stage, while gain maximizers focus on building the Y organization.

The most successful transformations usually are jointly led by a gain maximizer and a loss avoider, working together as partners.

How do you talk to each about XY? Gain maximizers will be more eager to talk about Y than XY. They may be reluctant to focus too much on the X → XY → Y transition, particularly if they perceive any suggestion of slowing the process down or reluctance to accept the inevitability of Y. So to talk to a gain maximizer about change, it is best to start by genuinely acknowledging the correctness of the Y vision. Then what works is to talk about ways to get to Y faster. The concept of XY has to be introduced to gain maximizers as a time-saver best practice that will accelerate true Y adoption. Create a vision of XY that they can connect to:

- XY is a faster route to Y that allows you to engage more people more quickly.

- XY is better because it is a truer picture of how people adopt change, and therefore people can more easily relate to an XY vision that to a pure-Y vision.

- XY is a cheaper way to demonstrate progress and success stories.

Stress the benefits (gains) that come from XY rather than the risks (loss) that might come from going directly to Y.

Alternatively, loss avoiders will be less eager to discuss Y on its own. They will be happy to discuss the X → XY → Y transition in detail, and in fact they will be suspicious of anyone whom they perceive as oversimplifying that change process. To talk to a loss avoider about change, begin by quickly acknowledging the Y vision. Then what works is to talk about other organizations that have made journeys to the same Y and to describe what they learned along the way. Describe the obstacles they encountered and how they overcame those challenges. The concept of XY should be introduced to loss avoiders as a risk reduction technique that minimizes the common pitfalls of change. Spell out the logic of an XY approach:

- XY is faster because it reduces resistance and dissension, which can slow change down.

- XY is better because it lowers risk by allowing smaller experiments and learning to occur.

- XY is cheaper because you don't have to replace all the initially unwilling X advocates with new Y hires.

As you can see, there are vast differences in how a salesperson should talk to gain maximizers and loss avoiders about change. Since a salesperson is increasingly a change management consultant, building fluency in both languages is critical.

Conclusion—Finding Smooth Air

We started this chapter by talking about the way in which many organizations freeze up during periods of change. Decisions are slowed, and innovation is reduced. Whether people are gain maximizers or loss avoiders, unless they are leading the change, they can feel overwhelmed by it. The role of the salesperson is to bring some order to what feels like chaos for the customer. That order can come from a simple vision of the future that makes sense or from examples of what other companies have done in similar situations. People want relief from the turbulence, but even more they want to know that the plane will still land safely.

CHAPTER 9

Disruption in Customer Buying Processes

Little kids love pony rides. At country fairs, they go round and round on a group of small ponies who walk in circles, tethered to a central post.

Salespeople love the predictability of customer buying cycles. They follow customers who go round and round taking the same five or six steps as they make buying decisions.

But pony rides come to an end, and so do buying cycles. As customers worldwide reengineer their buying processes, the idea of a closed-loop buying process is losing its validity and usefulness. As McKinsey & Company recently reported, "The funnel—the classic linear progression in which customers narrow their buying options as they advance from product awareness to purchase—is becoming a lot less relevant because customers are engaging in a much more iterative and dynamic decision journey."

Today buying is much more like a bucking bronco rodeo event than the pony ride that traditional buying cycles suggest. Lightning fast out of the gate, there is no predictable course once it starts, and it can come to a sudden stop. Multiple changes in direction are the only thing you can be sure of, and just when you think you are winning, the horse starts spinning and bucks you off in the dirt where you started.

The key to bronco riding is holding on tightly to the reins, using your free arm to help you keep your balance, leaning your body back, and grabbing the horse with your heels. What is the key to following your customer's unpredictable buying process today?

- Stay focused on what is best for the customer.

- Navigate the customer toward his or her destination.

- Rescue the customer from decision traps.

- Connect to multiple customer initiatives.

- Support customer stakeholders by reducing risk.

Hold on tightly, keep your balance, and don't let go. Spurs are not advised.

The Circular Buying Cycle

The highly useful idea of a buying cycle explains the stages that customers go through when making a purchase (see Figure 9.1). By recognizing the buying process stages, salespeople can adjust

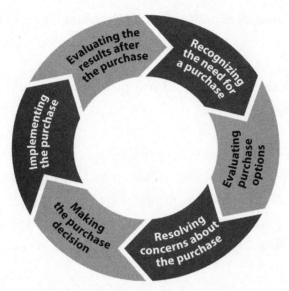

Figure 9.1   Traditional customer buying cycle.

their approach to provide customers with what they need at each stage—and they do have different needs at each stage.

Salespeople who focus more on their customer's buying process tend to be more successful than those who focus on their own sales process. The buying cycle is a model that helps salespeople maintain the right focus.

As the last chapter described, significant changes are occurring right now in the way customers make their buying decisions. Among these are:

- Decisions are being made more slowly.

- More stakeholders are involved in each decision.

- Risk assessment is becoming a bigger part of every decision process.

- Decisions often aren't made until the customer is out of time.

Implications are found throughout the stages of the traditional buying cycle:

- New customer priorities appear more quickly than ever before. Like the bronco rushing out of the gate, these come fast. That means that customers are "recognizing the need for a purchase" more frequently and more quickly, and they don't always move forward to "evaluating purchase options."

- Risk assessment is ever present. No one can afford for things to go wrong. That means that "resolving concerns about the purchase" occurs throughout the buying process.

- "Evaluating purchase options" never stops . . . even once an order is placed. How many times have you continued to Google alternatives to something you've purchased even though it is already on its way to you?

So what's happening here? And if the buying process is no longer cyclical, what does it look like?

Initiatives Trigger Buying Processes

A buying cycle begins when a customer recognizes the need for a purchase. Let's focus on major, occasional purchases for the moment. (We will come back to routine purchases later.) Today budgets are restricted and carefully scrutinized. This has always been true for capital budgets, but now it is true for operating expenses as well.

Today a decision to incur a major expense typically is the result of a strategic initiative. Why? Because the company believes the purchase will enable it to execute on one of its top strategic priorities. In fact, most strategic initiatives drive a number of major new purchases. Top salespeople long ago figured out that strategic initiatives are the best route to big budgets.

While there are certainly large purchases that are not tied to strategic initiatives, let's start with those that are, as shown in Figure 9.2.

Figure 9.2   The strategic initiative triggers the buying process.

Caught Up in the Decision Vortex

Let's look inside the life of a strategic initiative. From a distance it looks like something the executive team has defined and the organization then executes. But close up, it looks more like a television reality show: conflict, characters, repetition, and drama.

Here's the story of a strategic initiative:

The company realized that while it was renewing business at a good rate, its growth targets required that it improve its acquisition of new customers. New and nimble small players had entered its market, creating a more competitive climate. On top of that, a weakening economy in one of its main regions was now negatively impacting growth.

The executive team launched a strategic initiative focused on new client acquisition. The three components of the initiative focused on (1) a new CRM system, (2) training for the sales force, and (3) recruitment of additional business development salespeople. Leaders were assigned to each initiative component, created action plans, and began their work. Over three months, they made a series of decisions and began to execute on their purchases and hires. Several months later after a rigorous procurement process, they selected their CRM provider.

Then life happened. A bad quarter forced the company to review all expenses, including those that were to be used to get out of the hole it was in. This development slowed all purchases and hires, and it created a series of new meetings and discussions.

We call this a decision vortex. It's similar to what happens on a river. Just downstream of a large rock, water recirculates, being pulled upstream to the rock and downstream by the current. A whirlpool forms, making it hard to escape. If you're whitewater rafting and you get stuck in a vortex, it's not fun. But you can get out. You put all the weight you can on the upward side of the flow and push out to the edge of the whirlpool where the current is weaker.

Imagine the salesperson selling the CRM. She did all the right things: formed relationships with the company's executives, outlined the impact the CRM would have on the company's revenue growth, prepared an ROI analysis, and co-created her proposal with stakeholders. What she thought was a done deal was now in jeopardy (Figure 9.3).

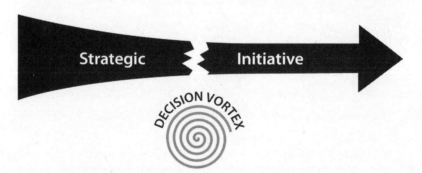

Figure 9.3   The strategic initiative is stalled by a decision vortex.

Multiple-Decision Vortices

In reality, strategic initiatives often encounter more than one vortex. Here's what continued to happen in the story above:

> A new CIO began studying a shift of company software and servers to the cloud, delaying the CRM purchase so that it could be integrated into that larger process. A competitor announced a major acquisition in an adjacent segment, leading people at the company to question whether they were pursuing the right strategy.

This is a fairly typical situation these days, with most strategic initiatives now looking something like the initiative pictured in Figure 9.4.

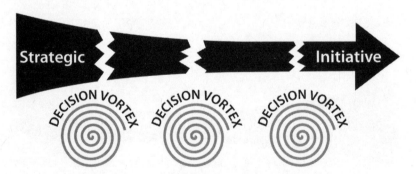

Figure 9.4 The strategic initiative is interrupted by multiple decision vortices.

Now what does that mean for our salesperson and the customer's buying cycle? As illustrated in Figure 9.5, it means that the buying process goes from being more or less a linear progression to a wandering path.

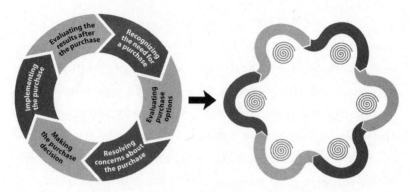

Figure 9.5   The nonlinear buying process emerges.

But that is actually an understatement. In reality, a vortex often sends a buying process back to an earlier stage. Sometimes it can jump a buying process forward. So it actually looks more like the hoofprints in a rodeo arena after a bucking bronco event, as Figure 9.6 shows.

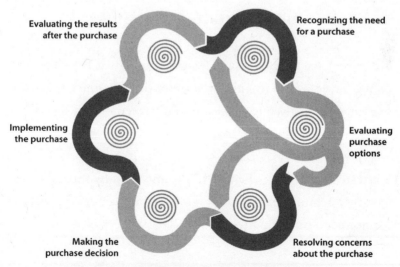

Figure 9.6   The decision vortices can send buyers back to earlier stages of decision making.

So a vortex in a strategic initiative can stall a buying cycle, send it backward, or send it forward. What sends it backward? Well, in the story above, the new CIO's desire to link several purchases together could send a buying process back from "evaluating purchase options" (or from any stage, really) to "recognizing the need for a purchase." What jumps it forward? Urgency. It becomes critical to execute quickly on a strategic initiative, perhaps as a response to a move by a competitor, as in the example above.

In Figure 9.6, we've shown what can happen when a decision vortex in a strategic initiative affects a customer who is "evaluating purchase options." But a decision vortex can affect any of the buying cycle stages, even "implementing the purchase." A change in the execution of a strategic initiative can stop, decelerate, delay, accelerate, or distort a buying cycle.

Multiple Strategic Initiatives

We've been focusing on a single strategic initiative, but most companies have three to five initiatives sponsored by the CEO at any one time. Typically, one of these initiatives is the most significant.

So you get something like this:

Strategic Initiative #1 (Figure 9.7) is impacted by three decision vortices, creating delays in execution and in the buying processes connected to that initiative.

Figure 9.7 The decision vortices delay execution.

Strategic Initiative #2 (Figure 9.8) is also impacted by three decision vortices, and after the third, it is stopped. The executives decide it won't have sufficient impact in the near term. All purchases related to this initiative are halted.

Figure 9.8 The decision vortices result in the initiative being stopped.

Strategic Initiative #3 (Figure 9.9) becomes more important because #2 was eliminated. A decision is made to invest more into it and to accelerate related purchases. It is not affected by the third vortex.

Figure 9.9 The decision vortex results in the initiative being accelerated.

Strategic Initiative #4 (Figure 9.10) is so critical to the CEO's agenda that it is not affected by any of the vortices.

Figure 9.10   The initiative continues without any decision vortex interruptions.

In later chapters, we will provide a set of ways that salespeople can manage and respond to decision vortices in their customer organizations. For now, let's look at what happens with decision vortices during times of X-to-Y change.

Purchases That Are Not Tied to Strategic Initiatives

Is every purchase linked to a strategic initiative? No. There are many products and services that a company needs to buy to stay in business and to produce its offerings. But even when, say, a company needs to buy 400 tons of raw materials each month to produce its products, those purchases can be affected by a decision vortex in a strategic initiative. If the vortex is big enough, it consumes everyone's attention. Budgets are frozen, and it's hard to get access to people to talk to them. Anything that can be delayed is delayed, and anything that can be cut is cut. This becomes particularly important if you are trying to displace an existing supplier. When there is a decision vortex in play, there's little chance of the customer making a major change. Of course, that can work to your advantage if your company is the existing supplier.

Whether we're talking about a raw materials purchase or other products and services that keep the customer's company operating (e.g., accounting services, office supplies, computers), buying decisions are affected by decision vortices in strategic initiatives. On these types of purchases, salespeople may have little chance of getting connected to executives or providing advice on the strategic initiative. They may only be connected to a single buyer and someone from procurement. What do you do in that case?

Here's the bad news for field salespeople: A lot of that type of transactional buying and selling is going to shift further to e-commerce. Unless salespeople can form relationships that allow them to identify and respond to the customer's nonprice interests, they will be displaced by technology. To prevent that, they must build a network of relationships in the customer organization. Going beyond the relationship with the buyer, they should be connected to users, stakeholders, and decision makers. From conversations with these people, they can stay apprised of the changing decision-making landscape and identify a wider range of nonprice elements that are important to the customer organization. In the ideal situation, these conversations lead to a way to support a strategic initiative, which can provide significant value to the customer and thereby relax pressure on pricing.

Decision Vortices During X-to-Y Change

We mentioned earlier that many top salespeople have had success linking their offerings to the big budgets that are attached to strategic initiatives. Almost all salespeople have felt the impact that changing strategic initiatives have on the budgets for their products or services. Far too many salespeople allow themselves to become victims of changing strategic initiatives. The only way to win the strategic initiative game is to become an advisor to the customers on how they can execute on their initiatives.

For a company undergoing X-to-Y change, some of the strategic initiatives will be dedicated to that change process. The first step for the salesperson is to focus on those initiatives connected to that X-to-Y change. That is where the most value can be provided.

The value the salesperson can provide is helping customers see the value of applying the $X \rightarrow XY \rightarrow Y$ approach. Often a strategic initiative focuses on working toward the Y future. By helping the customer organization see the benefit of the XY midpoint, the salesperson can help make those initiatives more successful. Of course, if the salesperson has access to the C-suite, that process is easier. However, in many cases, that access doesn't exist. In those situations, the salesperson should work with the buyers to focus on the execution of the initiatives, identifying ways to include an XY approach in how the initiative is carried out.

The other way the salesperson can apply XY thinking is when the decision vortices occur. It's too easy for a salesperson to tell his or her sales manager, "That deal is stalled. All budgets have been frozen," and move on to other opportunities. (If the salesperson has such a robust funnel that this opportunity should be deprioritized, that is a different situation, but in our experience that is rarely the case.) What can the salesperson do to help the customers out of the decision vortex? Help them see the bigger picture—the larger journey they are on. Help them see X and see Y and the path that connects the two, which includes the XY transition. By showing them you understand their journey, you will be brought into more business conversations and have a greater chance to impact their thinking and their buying decisions.

Conclusion—Expect a Rodeo

Given these more unpredictable buying behaviors, sellers need a larger number of opportunities if they hope to consistently exceed expectations. Sales leaders must respond to customers' new buying behaviors by adjusting their forecasts in order to avoid big negative surprises. More importantly, the whole sales organization needs to rethink how to manage the sales funnel and which sales activities are truly driving buying.

So welcome to your first rodeo. Don't expect a pony ride. Instead, if you assume twists, turns, hard stops, and flat-out sprints, you and your customer will have a much greater chance of winning.

CHAPTER 10

What Customers Expect from Salespeople

What if it turned out that salespeople were routinely leaving money on the table? Despite all the seemingly legitimate reasons for why selling is harder today, *what if* it turned out that customers are actually willing to buy more and at higher prices, if salespeople would engage them in ways that better aligned with what they truly want?

Those questions underlie an ongoing research study by BTS. Our data suggests some interesting conclusions:

- Customers want salespeople to help drive their overall business results.

- A significant gap exists between what customers want from salespeople and what the customers are getting.

- Many of the steps that sales leaders are taking to drive more revenue and profitability do not address this gap.

Is Sales Evolving?

Until about 30 years ago, selling was all about products. Customers had needs, and salespeople had products that filled those needs. Salespeople had to demonstrate great product knowledge and have the skills to identify their customers' needs and match those needs against their products. But starting around 20 years ago, almost every industry was invaded by providers with lower costs of labor or lower costs of raw materials, which drove down prices. Products became commoditized. At the same time, information about products became readily available on the web, so a salesperson wasn't offering value just by having good product knowledge.

In response to these phenomena, "solution selling" developed. Selling solutions meant wrapping sets of products and services together to solve the problems that customers encountered. The services included offerings such as financing, training, integration with existing systems, customized specifications, service, and support. Salespeople were trained not just to have great product knowledge, but also to find the "pain" in a customer's business process and propose a solution. The great thing about selling solutions was that the added services typically offered higher margins than the underlying products. But today everyone offers solutions, and just as with product selling, they have become commoditized.

A new way of selling has emerged. Today's leading sales forces have discovered that the way to stand out is to focus on *accelerating* the customer's desired business results. That means not just filling a need or solving a problem (though salespeople still have to be able to do that, too), but finding ways that their products or services can directly enable the customer to accelerate the desired performance. When salespeople practice this kind of selling, they are developing a deep understanding of the customer's overall business strategy, priorities, and objectives. Then they use all their company's capabilities (certainly products, services, and solutions, but also data, information, insights, expertise, and experience) to help that customer achieve the desired business results faster. (See Figure 10.1.)

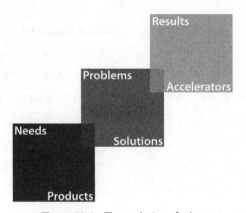

Figure 10.1   The evolution of sales.

BTS was the first to document this evolution in *The Mind of the Customer*, published by McGraw-Hill in 2006. Today the industry recognizes the shift that sales forces have begun to make. This new approach is referred to as "results selling," "value selling," "insight selling," "outcome selling," or as we call it, "accelerator selling." There is data that shows customers seek exactly this type of selling. Furthermore, our data shows that what customers want is more than just someone to challenge or provoke their thinking with new insights.

The Dangerous Middle

Have you ever revisited a favorite restaurant and discovered it to be not as good as it once was? It's a disappointment. The food isn't the way you remember it. The service seems to have deteriorated. There aren't as many diners in the place. Finally, you force yourself to acknowledge that it is on the decline, and you vow not to come back.

Many sales leaders have spent the last decade taking their salespeople to a restaurant called Solution Selling. And that restaurant is slowly going out of business. Let us explain.

In the last few years, new buying patterns have emerged. This shift threatens the approach that many sales leaders take.

During the global financial crisis of 2007–2009, business-to-business customers changed their buying behavior. What they began to say is, "If you can truly accelerate the achievement of my desired business results, I will buy more from you and pay a premium for your offering. However, anything short of that I will treat as a commodity and run through my procurement organization." The split that appeared is shown in Figure 10.2.

One of the biggest impacts of that split is that customers now treat solutions the same way they treat products. In fact, they attach no value to added features that they don't desire. Essentially, they seek to buy solutions at product prices, which

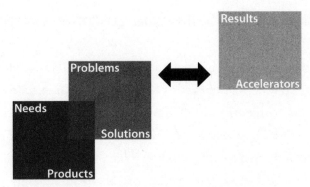

Figure 10.2   Accelerator selling is now treated differently by customers from product and solution selling.

they can do because supplier competition is severe in this solutions space.

This development puts suppliers in an awkward position. They are now selling fairly complex packaged offerings at prices no better than they get on the core products underlying those solutions. That has killed margins.

A similar situation has confronted casual dining chains in the United States. The casual dining segment, defined in the United States by restaurants like Chili's, Applebee's, Red Lobster, and Olive Garden, is in trouble. Customer traffic to this segment has declined in 9 of the last 13 years. What's happening? Fast casual restaurants, like Chipotle and Panera, are offering better, more natural food faster and at a slightly lower cost. All that's missing is table service. Traditional casual dining chains have responded by reducing prices and fighting each other for share in a declining market.

This is what it's like to defend the middle, in this case between fast food on one side and fine dining on the other. The middle is a difficult space to occupy these days.

What Kind of Selling Do Customers Want?

Our research contains both quantitative and qualitative elements. BTS has conducted hundreds of interviews with executive-level customers to identify the behaviors that customers seek from salespeople. These behaviors were used to develop a survey instrument to quantify the validity of the research across different industries and geographies. At the core of our survey is the opportunity for customers to choose their preference across 15 behavioral dimensions. Each of the behavioral dimensions has a unique expression across three distinct types of selling: product selling, solution selling, and accelerator selling, as shown in Table 10.1.

Product Selling	Solution Selling	Accelerator Selling
Focuses discussions on the **product or service needs** the customer needs to fulfill	Focuses discussions on **specific problems or issues** the customer needs to resolve	Focuses discussions on the **business results** the customer's company needs to achieve

Table 10.1   The Evolution of Selling

During the survey, respondents are not exposed to this model, and the model is not apparent from the way the questions are asked. In fact, the behaviors that align to each type of selling are randomized, so that the respondents cannot easily detect the underlying pattern. The survey has now been conducted with 638 customers worldwide.

Beyond Solution Selling

One way to assess the data is to look at overall averages to determine where in the continuum of selling customer preferences emerge.

Our data shows that a clear majority of customers want an approach where the salesperson is working to accelerate their overall business results, not just solve problems or fill product needs. Solution selling is insufficient to reach these customers, and product selling does not connect with their requirements. Customers seek salespeople who have moved on from only discussing business process problems and solutions to discussing the overall business results the customer's company is trying to achieve.

Our interviews, and a longer body of earlier research we conducted, suggest that the customers' desired approach is shifting toward accelerator selling over time, as you can see in Figure 10.3. Most sales forces we encounter are also moving toward accelerator selling, but at a lagging speed.

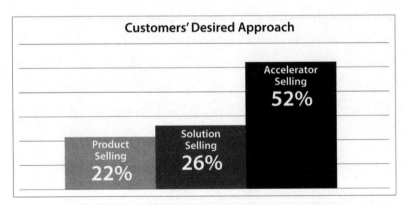

Figure 10.3   Most customers desire a selling approach that accelerates the overall business results they seek to achieve.

The data suggests a bigger issue that is directly affecting the ability of companies to grow revenue today. The sales approaches that customers want are not what they are getting. Customers tell us they would buy more, and at higher prices, if they could get salespeople to sell in a way that aligns with the way they want to buy.

The graph in Figure 10.4 shows what customers seek and what they see.

Figure 10.4   Customers are not getting the type of selling approaches they seek.

What customers typically encounter are salespeople who focus on filling product needs or, in some cases, salespeople who focus on finding and solving problems. The vacuum between what customers want and what they are getting represents a significant competitive opportunity for sales forces that can shift the way they sell to better align with what customers want.

The Value Gap

The difference between the sales behavior that customers seek and what they actually get from salespeople can be considered a *value gap*. In Figure 10.5, we focus on the value gap for customers who prefer accelerator selling because this is where the greatest potential exists for increasing revenue and margins. But it should be noted that it is also beneficial to better align sales activity and behavior with the desires of customers who prefer product or solution selling. Not only will it increase customer loyalty; it will also likely reduce the cost of sales.

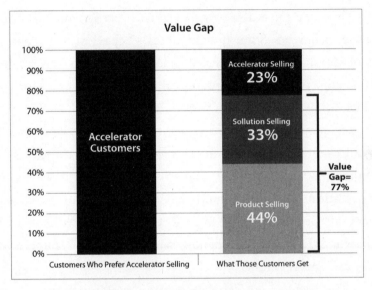

Figure 10.5   Only a small percentage of accelerator customers get the sales behaviors they seek.

Of the customers who prefer an accelerator-selling approach, only 23 percent typically see those behaviors from salespeople. Note that the difference between the graph in Figure 10.4 and the graph in Figure 10.5 is that the one in Figure 10.5 looks only at the customers who prefer accelerator selling and the behaviors they report seeing.

The remaining customers who prefer an accelerator-selling approach get product-selling behaviors (44 percent) or solution-selling behaviors (33 percent). This *value gap* translates into lost revenue and lower margins for sales forces that are misaligned with their customers.

Another way of expressing the value gap is that 77 percent of customers who prefer to be sold to in a way that accelerates their overall business results are not being sold to the way they want to buy.

The value gap is also useful as a benchmark to measure component behaviors. Some individual sales behaviors have a larger value gap than the overall set of behaviors; others have a smaller value gap. This ranking process can help sales forces prioritize which behaviors to address first.

The majority of customers want their salespeople to understand their business objectives, priorities, opportunities, and challenges, which implies that these customers have higher expectations for salesperson behavior. These customers clearly want salespeople to behave in a way that is aligned with accelerator selling. They need salespeople to help them make connections they can't make on their own.

What becomes critical, then, is first identifying those customers who seek accelerator selling and then closing the value gap, ensuring that the salespeople who serve them behave in the ways these customers prefer. When that happens, these customers buy more and at higher margins. When this does not happen, customers will either seek lower prices or turn to competitors.

Do Sales Leaders Know What to Do?

The implications of the value gap can be seen in longer sales cycles, more price pressure, and less customer loyalty.

The critical point is this: salespeople who want success in today's marketplace must shift beyond a product-driven conversation with the majority of customers who clearly want a different approach. Most sales leaders know that at some level. But here's what is different: shifting to a problem-finding, solution-selling approach is not enough. In fact, it may be the wrong direction entirely, as the number of customers seeking a solution-selling approach is actually diminishing.

Salespeople who want to succeed in today's business environment need to align with their most valuable customers by having business conversations that go beyond today's challenges. They must discuss more than the potential implications of a purchase on the customers' business. These business conversations must explore the customers' own customers, their value proposition to those customers, the trends in their markets, and the metrics they use to measure success. Sellers who are able to close the value gap take the time to understand their customers holistically. They have the business acumen to turn their understanding into insights and their insights into results.

The failure to close this value gap—the difference between product conversations and business conversations—is driving longer sales cycles, greater discounting, more frequent customer churn, and slower acquisition of new customers.

With the best of intentions, what many sales leaders do when they see those developments is twofold:

1. They double down on driving activity metrics, hoping that more sales activity will compensate for fewer deals at lower margins that take longer to close.

2. They initiate a back-to-basics approach or "blocking-and-tackling" focus that actually reinforces a set of

product-selling behaviors that further misalign salespeople with what customers want.

The good news is that there are simple, specific, and high-impact actions that salespeople can take instead.

What to Do

When customers are asked to choose the sales behaviors they value most from salespeople, the top behaviors are:

1. Demonstrates knowledge of customer's business objectives, priorities, opportunities, and challenges

2. Demonstrates an appropriate sense of urgency by responding quickly and diligently

3. Demonstrates an understanding of the customer's business and marketplace dynamics

Focusing on these three behaviors will enable you to close the value gap and align with what customers expect. All three behaviors are characteristic of an accelerator-selling approach.

For the first desired behavior, salespeople must research their customer's overall business before a client interaction, ask smart, business-focused questions, and possess enough business acumen to carry on a business conversation. When sales leaders mention that salespeople need to sell higher or that they struggle to get executive access, it is often because these salespeople simply do not have the business acumen or conversational skills to engage in a meaningful executive interaction.

Not long ago, a 24-hour response time was acceptable to most customers. Those days are gone. In today's mobile-enabled world, customers expect answers within the hour. That's often because they have to get back to their bosses within the hour. Even over the weekend. They also want to know that the salesperson is helping to move their buying process forward.

Finally, accelerating the customer's overall business results means bringing to bear all of a selling company's resources to help the customer succeed. That means not only products and solutions but data, information, insights, expertise, and experience to help that customer achieve the desired business results faster. Sales leaders who take an inside-out view call this cross-selling. Here you have customers saying they want cross-selling, as long as it helps them achieve their desired business results faster.

An initial focus on these three high-impact behaviors will go a long way to closing the value gap. More broadly, and over the longer term, closing the value gap requires sales leaders to look differently at the behaviors and knowledge they seek from their teams.

What Is Changing Now

We are at a key moment in the evolution of selling. As product selling and solution selling split off from accelerator selling (call it "conscious uncoupling" if you like), there are two major implications.

It is quickly becoming conventional wisdom that customers are delaying the involvement of salespeople in their buying processes. We are always suspicious of conventional wisdom, and caution certainly applies here. These delays in salesperson involvement are increasingly true for product buyers and even for solution buyers. But for accelerator purchases (and particularly those that are linked to the implementation of a strategic initiative), we are actually seeing more early outreach to providers to access insights, consulting, data, benchmarking, and other advice.

Another piece of conventional wisdom is that the Internet has shifted power from sellers to buyers. More than 35 years ago, Michael Porter identified the bargaining power of suppliers and the bargaining power of customers as two of his five forces that famously determine the level of competition in an industry. In 1998, Porter announced that the Internet "dramatically increases available information, shifting bargaining power to buyers."

Much of the struggle that salespeople have faced over the past decade could be attributed to this shift in market power from dominant suppliers to newly knowledge-rich sellers. But this ongoing seesaw ride between buyers and sellers is not over yet.

The best salespeople in the world today increasingly leverage the Internet to become knowledge-rich sellers. They access information about their individual buyers (through LinkedIn and other social media), obtain the latest information on the buying company's financial performance, download the buying company's presentations on its strategic initiatives from investor relations web pages, and review Glassdoor to get inside tips on what is going on inside the firm.

It's a fallacy to think that the Internet only works in favor of buyers. Salespeople just need to learn to leverage it as nimbly as buyers do.

Accelerator Selling in the X-to-Y World

The next wave of accelerator selling is enabling companies to accomplish major change. Remember, accelerator selling is all about helping customers achieve their desired business results. For companies moving from any X to any Y, the role of the accelerator salesperson is to help them get to Y faster.

Consistent with everything we've been saying throughout this book, the best approach to getting to Y faster is to develop and communicate clarity about what the XY world looks like. The role of the salesperson is (1) to help the customer understand the value of the $X \rightarrow XY \rightarrow Y$ approach, as opposed to an $X \rightarrow Y$ process, and (2) to help the customer define both XY and Y.

One of the hurdles to accelerator selling generally has been that it requires a level of business acumen that historically salespeople did not require. Sales forces did not necessarily try to recruit salespeople with business acumen, and until recently sales forces did not invest in training salespeople with those skills. As we mentioned earlier in this chapter, accelerator selling requires that you understand your customers' business drivers in depth. To provide the added value required during a period of major change, that business acumen becomes even more important. For salespeople to be treated as informal change consultants—which is the role that will best position them for the future—they must be able to talk about the business implications of each element of change. How does the decline in the customer's X business affect margins? What is the impact on market share of getting to Y faster? How does the XY phase affect employee engagement?

This all sounds hard and complicated, and it is, but the best salespeople in the world are doing this right now, and it is what differentiates them with their customers. The profile of a star salesperson today is someone who provides significant value by helping customers through change and in return becomes the preferred supplier for that customer.

In the following chapters, we will expand further on the steps a salesperson can take to be a true accelerator in an X-to-Y world.

Conclusion—A Prediction for the Future

In 10 years, we believe, there will be half as many salespeople as there are today. Half as many. But the half that remains will earn double what they do today. Why? Because the remaining half will be primarily accelerator sellers. They will be generating true results for their customers and for the companies they work for. Their customers will pay higher prices to work with them and buy more from their companies.

The buying of products will increasingly shift to e-commerce platforms. There will be a reduced need for salespeople, particularly field salespeople. During what will continue to be a long transition, the need for inside salespeople (who bridge the gap between e-commerce and field reps) will increase.

The lesson for field salespeople is this: become proficient at accelerator selling or begin looking for a new career.

PART 3

Salespeople—
Selling Change

CHAPTER 11

Great Selling: Navigation Skills

W e've all been there: staring blankly at a vast display of televisions inside a consumer electronics store. So many choices! Are there meaningful differences? Which is the right one for me? How do I get the most value for my money? How do I make the right decision? Will I make the right decision? Looking at web reviews on my phone, I still find it impossible to determine the best option for me. Maybe it's just easier to go home and deal with this another time.

This quandary is not just a situation in which consumers find themselves. Businesses face the same circumstances every day. Even for major purchases, businesses today are confronting an unexpected wealth of choices. From the point of view of the various sellers offering their products and services to the company, there may be important differentiators and multiple levels of value. But to the people in the company making the buying decision, the choice can feel much the same as the consumer facing that wall of televisions.

As salespeople, we often think of ourselves presenting a great product or solution to the customer. But customers see this completely differently. They see too many choices without clear differentiators. At some point it becomes easiest to just make a choice based on price. No one will question that.

Becoming the Salesperson that Customers Seek

The research that BTS has conducted with 638 buyers globally shows that customers do not want to make their purchase decision just based on price. What they want are salespeople who will help them make the right choice that maximizes the overall value equation.

Constant change and uncertainty have exhausted buyers; the global economy has made every major purchasing decision seem like life or death. Customers today need salespeople to help reduce complexity and guide them through the chaos on their path from X to Y. While this relationship requires trust, trust alone isn't enough. Customers want help narrowing down the options and making the right buying decision.

That is why we think it is time to move beyond the concept of becoming the customer's *trusted advisor*. The idea of becoming a trusted advisor is about building the right customer relationship defined by credibility, reliability, and intimacy, all with a focus on the customer rather than the salesperson. While still true today, that concept lacks a critical component that customers now expect from salespeople.

Much has been written in recent years about the need for salespeople to provoke or challenge their customers. There's a lot of truth to that within the trusted advisor concept, particularly when it's done with genuine humility and curiosity rather than arrogance and condescension. But our research suggests that's only a piece of the pie, not the entire pie.

What customers today want is a salesperson with navigation skills. They have a destination in mind. Typically, that destination (the vision for Y) is defined by the business goals they want to achieve and the targets they need to hit, as well as the dynamics of their industry. They may or may not know the best path to take, but they will engage with someone they believe will guide them toward that destination. They seek salespeople who understand their industry terrain, can chart new trails based on their individual priorities, and know when to take a shortcut and when it is best to take the long way around. In this view, the successful accelerator salesperson is a *navigator*.

How to Use Navigation Techniques

Think about what navigators provide on a journey. They have a clear understanding of the desired destination. They know where you want to go. And they have been to that destination before. In fact, they are experts on the multiple ways of getting to that destination. Good navigators know where obstacles lie along the path as well as how to avoid them. They know where the shortcuts exist. More than that, they are also calm and in control, with a clear and compelling vision of how the journey will go.

What does this mean for salespeople? How can you develop navigation skills?

Navigation Skills

As Figure 11.1 shows, navigating the sales journey is a three-step process.

Navigation Skills

Figure 11.1   Three skills of navigation.

Navigation Step 1: Identify the Destination

First, you have to gain a full understanding of the customer's intended destination. That destination can be thought of as the customer's *desired result* and can be communicated by the customer in multiple ways:

- Vision of success

- Goals

- Metrics or key performance indicators (KPIs)

Becoming an expert on the customer's desired result means two things: (1) asking the right questions and (2) having sufficient business acumen to understand the answers. It's one thing to learn that the customer wants to improve inventory turns. But it's something else to understand why, know what to ask next, and know what to do. By showing customers that you understand their destination and starting point holistically and by making it clear that you are genuinely interested in their results, you begin to earn the right to provide the customer with navigation assistance.

In an environment of customer change, applying navigation skills requires you to fully understand the customer's vision of the Y destination. Y could be a new go-to-market strategy, a new approach to manufacturing and production, a different way of organizing distribution, or a reorganization of people and reporting structures. It could be a merger integration or a significant product launch. It won't be hard to figure out what Y is because everyone will be talking about it. What's a bit harder, but possible with work and the right questions, is deeply understanding the customer's vision for achieving Y. That takes, in part, familiarity with the metrics that the customer will use to measure the success of Y.

Navigation Step 2: Clarify the Path

The second step for salespeople who want to use navigation skills is to offer expertise along the journey to the destination. That, too, begins with questions. Few customers are standing still, waiting for their journey to begin. Most have already begun the process. So the salesperson must ask questions about what they have done so far and where they have been. This includes topics such as:

- Current strategic initiatives

- Marketplace trends they are leveraging

- Innovations and improvements they are making

Applying navigation techniques also means understanding how the customer organization views the X starting point. There is no path without both X and Y.

Some of the greatest value that salespeople offer is something that most salespeople don't even recognize: their awareness of how other similar companies are executing. Providing expertise on the journey involves sharing insights about what other companies have discovered along the way. That doesn't mean sharing anything that is proprietary to those companies, but it does mean saying things like, "Typically, when companies shift their servers to the cloud, they take one of three approaches. Here are the benefits and disadvantages of each approach . . ."

This is also the time to challenge traditional thinking and offer insights. Many times, great salespeople can highlight what the customer sees as constraints but are actually self-imposed limitations. The salesperson can recommend alternative paths to success that the customer, who is just too close to the day-to-day realities, cannot see. The key to doing this in a way that the customer will appreciate is to be humble: ask questions; offer hypotheses; show empathy.

Next the salesperson has to advise the customer on the path from X to Y. The recommendations should incorporate what the company is already doing and include the steps it should take to get to its results faster. This is when the salesperson begins to talk about products and services. In complex sales, we often recommend that no products or services be discussed in the first two interactions. The first interaction is all about understanding the customer's desired destination. The second is about the route options. In the third, the salesperson can offer recommendations for the path—a proposal.

The proposal should lay out the way that the sellers' offerings contribute to the X → XY → Y journey and should include options. It should document the value of defining the XY space and how that will actually accelerate progress toward the Y destination. Typically, the benefits of defining XY are:

- Creates a short-term picture of success

- Represents a smaller, more manageable increment of change

- Reduces resistance to change

- Reduces risk

- Maintains the commitment to achieving Y in the same time horizon

Chapter 8 provided more detail on describing to customers the advantages of focusing on an XY execution approach.

Navigation Step 3: Measure Progress

Chapter 10 explained how customers today will buy more and at higher prices if by doing so they will genuinely accelerate the achievement of their desired business results. What salespeople often fail to do is to demonstrate progress on the metrics that customers care about. So the journey must include a way of measuring progress on those metrics. More specifically, it must incorporate performance metrics that will be used to measure the purchase's contributions to X, to Y, and to XY.

In many situations, the salespeople disappear once the sale is closed, handing off the "service" aspect to others in their company. And while the implementation of the purchase almost inevitably requires such a handoff, the best salespeople do not disappear. As customer navigators, they know they must be present at key points throughout the implementation process. Their main role during this stage is to help the customer interpret the progress being made, as well as ensure that any obstacles impeding progress are removed. When progress against the metrics is measured consistently and the original promises from the sales process are being met, salespeople are setting up their next sales. They are uncovering new needs and building trust that they are the right partners.

The right way to navigate at this stage is to assume responsibility for measuring and reporting progress on the journey. That process starts with working collaboratively with customers to determine the metrics to be measured. This is best done during the sales process, incorporated into the proposal, and confirmed at regular intervals. These steps are hugely valuable in creating differentiation between salespeople who are committed to fulfilling the customers' desired business results and those who are simply there to solve a problem or fill a product need. Salespeople should also guide their customers to the best measurement techniques. When they take the lead in preparing the periodic measurement reports, salespeople reinforce their roles as true partners in their customers' desired outcomes.

The converse of this situation happens all too frequently: during the implementation, a customer stakeholder challenges the value being created, and without clear measures of progress, doubt begins to infuse the customer organization.

Conclusion—Getting to Desired Results Faster, for Everyone

When a salesperson uses navigation skills, everyone benefits: The customer gets to the desired destination (or results) faster. The selling company gets paid not only for its products or services, but both for the added value its salesperson provides by guiding the customer through the implementation process and for demonstrable, clearly measured results. And the salesperson benefits by deepening the relationship with the customer and becoming an essential partner on the customer's journey.

Navigation skills are what will help you be a successful accelerator. The accelerator salesperson is all about getting the customers to the desired results faster. Navigation skills help you do that by assisting the client with identifying the destination, clarifying the path, and measuring progress.

CHAPTER 12

Great Selling:
Core Selling Behaviors

H ere's an insight: *accelerator selling is not all about insights.* There is a role for insights in accelerator selling. The customer wants salespeople to offer a compelling vision of the future and a point of view on how the customer's company needs to prepare for that future. And the customer wants that vision anchored in a deep understanding of the trends that are shaping the market, the major industry challenges, the performance of the top competitors, the position each player takes for itself, and the ways new entrants are reshaping the competitive game. The salespeople must be able to explain how their offering best prepares the customer for that future.

Customers in our research base say they want salespeople to offer these insights not with arrogance but with humility. Instead of approaches where the salesperson challenges or provokes the customer, what customers want is a salesperson who asks smart questions first. Yes, the salesperson should have done the necessary homework and obtained all publicly available information elsewhere. But executive buyers in particular want to be engaged in a conversation about what the future could bring. They do not want a salesperson telling them they must do a certain thing if they want to succeed going forward.

There are other issues with selling approaches that overrely on insights. First, insight-driven selling drives longer sales cycles, slower funnel velocity, and lower hit rates. These insight-driven sales often have no budgets allocated to them, require extensive stakeholder deliberation, and result in "no-decision" outcomes.

Second, insight selling is difficult to execute. Only a small percentage of salespeople have the capacity to create insights, even after training. As a result, many companies have their marketing departments create the insights, and they train their salespeople to customize those insights for each customer. Marketing-driven insights, however, have to be generated constantly to be current, and marketing's natural distance from the customer can make those insights less relevant. Getting this right is possible, but it is a large and expensive undertaking.

The way to use insights well is to keep everything simple. Stay focused on the salesperson and the customer. Insights have to show that:

- The salesperson understands what's important to each buyer at each customer organization and what results each buyer wants to achieve.

- The salesperson can help the customer get to those desired results faster.

BTS has identified the core behaviors of accelerator selling, of which insights is one component. In the next section, we'll explore those behaviors.

How to Be an Accelerator Salesperson

There is a fairly specific set of knowledge and behaviors required to be a successful accelerator. Required knowledge starts with business acumen. That can come from industry experience (particularly in the customer's industry), from training, from learning on the job, or from educational background. Without business acumen, the salesperson cannot fully appreciate the customer's business context and the results the customer is executing toward.

Knowledge

Business acumen is the foundation that drives several types of knowledge that customers in our research tell us are critical today:

- Knowledge of the customer's business

- Knowledge of the customer's industry

- Knowledge of the salesperson's own company

To be an accelerator, the salesperson must also have the product and technical knowledge required to define the customer journey—what the customer will do or deploy to accomplish its objectives.

Behaviors

We have identified the seven critical elements of accelerator selling. They are shown in the "periodic table" in Figure 12.1. The first elements describe what salespeople need to do.

While there are other important categories of knowledge that must be demonstrated for customers, the one type of knowledge that is required for accelerator selling (and less important in product or solution selling) is:

* **Customer understanding.** Demonstrating deep knowledge of the customer's business and industry.

The next row of the table shows the four steps that should be included in every customer interaction:

* **Plan.** Preparing for the customer interaction (not filling out a fancy, complicated worksheet, but spending sufficient time

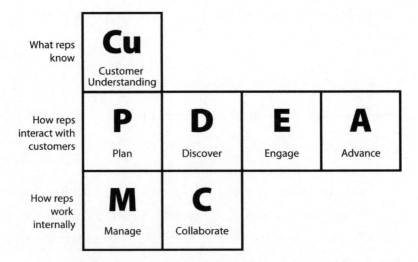

Figure 12.1   Periodic table of accelerator-selling behaviors.

to do the necessary research, set objectives for the meeting, and create an agenda).

- **Discover.** Asking questions that get deep inside the customer's view of the business.

- **Engage.** Rather than presenting, involving the customer in a compelling discussion of the value the salesperson's company offers, ideally one where the offering is co-created with the customer.

- **Advance.** Moving the customer to the next stage in the buying process, no matter where that customer is in the buying cycle. Of course, this includes closing.

There are two final sales behaviors that are critical for accelerator sellers but take place out of the view of the customer:

- **Manage.** Creating strategies to manage opportunities, accounts, and territories.

- **Collaborate.** Working with others in the selling company on behalf of the customer.

A more detailed description of what "great" looks like for each behavior is provided in Table 12.1.

The good news is that the seven behaviors above can all be learned. Now here's the bad news: our research shows a significant gap on all seven behaviors between what customers want from their salespeople and what they receive. As described in Chapter 10, the data suggests that 77 percent of customers who prefer to be sold to in a way that accelerates their overall business

Accelerator Value Element	What "Great" Looks Like
Customer Understanding: What you know about your customer's business	• Demonstrate you know your customer's: ○ Customers ○ Value proposition to its customers ○ Marketplace dynamics ○ Business objectives ○ Strategic priorities ○ Opportunities ○ Challenges
Plan: What you do before a customer interaction	• For every customer interaction: ○ Have an objective. Make the objective customer-focused (rather than sales focused). ○ Have an agenda. ○ Have provocative questions prepared. ○ Prepare an insight that respects the uniqueness of this customer's business and priorities. ○ Consider alternative scenarios for what could happen during the discussion and how to proceed.
Discover: How you determine what customers value	• Center discussions on the business results that your customer's company needs to achieve. • Ask provocative questions based on your knowledge of the customer's business environment. • Ask about your customer's buying process, stakeholders, and buying criteria.
Engage: How you articulate the value of your offerings	• Create solutions with clear cause and effect relationships between the offerings and business results. • Quantify the value of the offerings by showing how they impact metrics that are important to your customer. • Co-create innovative solutions with your customer to maximize business impact and stakeholder support. • Develop an extensive network of relationships within the customer organization.
Advance: How you move the sale forward	• Demonstrate an appropriate sense of urgency by responding quickly and diligently. • Help your customer think through difficult business challenges or take advantage of unseen opportunities. • Negotiate collaboratively by exploring interests and suggesting options. • Evaluate the business impact of the purchase after the implementation.
Manage: How you build your overall book of business	• Take a comprehensive and strategic approach. • Consider all the potential opportunities and all the potential buyers. • Focus on ensuring your customer's business success (rather than just on your sales goals).
Collaborate: How you work with others in your organization	• Fully leverage other individuals and resources in your own company to get the results your customers need.

Table 12.1   Description of "Great" Accelerator-Selling Behaviors

results are instead being sold to in a way that is focused on products and problems.

Too much of today's sales training is locked in a legacy worldview that no longer is relevant. While sales managers seek to inculcate new reps with the training concepts they once learned, many of those concepts have shrinking relevance today. Training people to "handle objections," "identify champions," and "find pain" (just a few examples) does not provide reps with the skills they need to be navigators and to demonstrate the behaviors that customers seek today.

What Is Different for Key Account Managers

Many salespeople are assigned to a single large account. They may be called "key account managers," "strategic account managers," "global account managers," or something else. For simplicity here, we're going to call them key account managers (KAMs).

It has now become commonplace to say that great salespeople don't always make great sales managers. But guess what? Great salespeople don't always make great KAMs either. KAMs require many of the same behaviors that are required of other salespeople in today's sales environment, plus an additional set of behaviors that are critical in guiding teams to serve key accounts. There are 12 relevant behaviors. First we will list those; then we'll assess where KAMs are typically weak and strong.

In Figure 12.2, the seven behaviors on the left are the critical behaviors for accelerator salespeople that we described above. The five behaviors on the right (in the black keys) are additional behaviors relevant to KAMs.

What Great KAM Behavior Looks Like

Critical Salesperson Behaviors	Additional KAM Behaviors
Customer Understanding Demonstrating deep knowledge of the customer's overall business	**Company Understanding** Demonstrating deep knowledge of how their own business makes money and understanding the key tradeoffs that drive revenue growth and profitability
Plan Preparing for customer interactions	**Portfolio** Working with others in the organization to create unique offerings to meet customers' business needs
Discover Asking results-focused questions to determine business priorities	
Engage Demonstrating value in a customer-centered manner	**Lead** Guiding the key account team to its goals
Advance Helping the customer move to the next stage of their buying process	**Orchestrate** Organizing team activities to drive a single coordinated approach to the account
Manage Creating and executing account, opportunity, and territory plans	**Execute** Ensuring successful achievement of each element of the account plan
Collaborate Leveraging internal resources on behalf of the customer	

Figure 12.2   Definition of "great" for KAMs.

Our review of KAM programs at 15 major global sales forces suggests that KAMs fall short in particular behaviors. On average, most KAM organizations have the biggest gaps in the following subcomponents of each behavior category:

Customer Understanding

- Understanding the changing market dynamics affecting the customer's business

Engage

- Engaging executives in customer organizations

- Assembling and presenting business cases to executives

Advance

- Using strategic customer understanding and business cases to move opportunities forward through the customer's buying process

Company Understanding

- Creating business cases that demonstrate the value to the KAM's own company of making changes to prices, resources, or customization on behalf of a specific customer

When you examine the gaps identified above, two themes emerge: dynamic business acumen and business-case agility (see Figure 12.3). Today these two abilities are what distinguish great KAMs from average KAMs. And look carefully: it's all about change, about "dynamic" and "agility." The rate of change in customer organizations is creating a need for KAMs to understand what is changing in a customer's business (particularly those X-to-Y shifts) and to be able to present business cases on the spot in rapidly changing situations. Let's explore those themes further.

KAM Behaviors and Gaps

Behaviors All Salespeople Need	Additional Behaviors KAMs Need	The Key Gaps for KAMs
• Customer Understanding • Plan • Discover • Engage • Advance • Manage • Collaborate	• Company Understanding • Portfolio • Lead • Orchestrate • Execute	• Dynamic Business Acumen • Business-Case Agility

Figure 12.3   Gaps in KAM behavior.

Dynamic Business Acumen

Traditionally, business acumen is defined as understanding how a company makes money. It includes knowledge of the drivers of growth, profitability, and cash flow; knowledge of the company's markets; and knowledge of the interrelationships within the business. When we work with salespeople to build business acumen, we typically revise this definition to reflect the customer-facing nature of salespeople. In the sales world, business acumen means knowledge of the drivers of *customer* growth, profitability, and cash flow; knowledge of the *customer's* markets; and knowledge of the interrelationships within the *customer's* business.

Here's what is critical for key account managers and what we mean by *dynamic business acumen*: knowledge of how the drivers of customer growth, profitability, and cash flow *are changing*; knowledge of how the customer's markets *are changing*; and knowledge of how the interrelationships within the customer's business *are changing*. Without becoming an expert on what is changing, salespeople cannot assist with the customer's X → Y transition.

As we wrote in Chapter 9, frequent changes in customers' strategic initiatives are impacting customer buying cycles in significant ways. Understanding those frequent changes is critical for a KAM who is accountable for dozens (or hundreds) of individual sales to one customer organization at any one time.

There is a huge upside to having true dynamic business acumen: access to more C-suite executives. While basic business acumen is a ticket to entry these days, it alone will not get the executive meeting. (It just ensures the meeting will go relatively well if the meeting is obtained.) Dynamic business acumen can actually drive greater C-level access because executives are always eager to talk with someone knowledgeable about what is changing in their company and their industry. This is particularly true if salespeople can convert their understanding into an insight that has value to the executive.

The easiest ways for a KAM to provide insights to executives are to (1) understand current marketplace trends and discuss the likelihood and severity of their potential impacts on this company and (2) provide realistic options, or execution paths, and describe the advantages and disadvantages of each. Promising one or both of those to an executive will almost always result in a meeting.

Building dynamic business acumen capabilities also enables the second success factor: business-case agility.

Business-Case Agility

There are two reasons that salespeople prepare business cases: First, they sometimes need to defend to the customer the value of what they are proposing. (In these cases, shorter justifications work best, with detailed appendixes if needed.) Second, salespeople sometimes need to present a business case internally on behalf of a customer when they are trying to do something that requires going beyond standard procedures. Often they are asking for additional resources for the customer, extensive customization of the solution, or further discounts.

Generally, salespeople are weak in preparing business cases. They typically don't get training on how to prepare a business case; there are few if any good models to work from; and broadly speaking, people with strong analytic skills are often not attracted to sales roles. This skill gap is usually balanced with other strengths and talents, and it does not significantly impact the salesperson's ability to sell. However, with those in KAM roles, the ability to prepare and present a business case becomes more important, both because of the level at which they are operating and because of the sheer number of sales they are responsible for.

Not only do KAMs need to be proficient with creating and presenting business cases; they need to do so with agility—adapting business cases to changing situations:

- **Quick changes on the fly.** KAMs must be able to adapt their business cases to the dynamic customer situations and markets we described earlier. There often isn't time to go back to the office and work with a colleague or manager. It has to happen in the moment.

- **Presentations without preparation.** KAMs can be called upon at any time to present a business case. They can't count on time to prepare and rehearse. In these sudden presentations, it's critical that they not get flustered; they have to demonstrate confidence. Tentativeness will make customers hesitant.

Dynamic business acumen and business-case agility will improve the ability of KAMs to demonstrate customer understanding at a strategic level, enable better conversations with and presentations to executives, advance customer decision processes, and allow for better internal decisions in support of key accounts.

Next we'll leave the world of key accounts and look at prospecting, for all types of salespeople.

Behaviors that Make Prospecting Successful

One of the most common questions we get from salespeople and sales leaders is, "What can we do differently to improve our prospecting efforts?" The answer lies not in increased call activity levels, not in search engine optimization, and certainly not in buying those e-mail lists you get offered in spam messages. Surprisingly, the answer comes down to age-old human wisdom: serve other people before expecting them to do something for you.

Much of what we describe below applies to growing existing accounts as well as to prospecting. To keep things simple, we'll discuss prospecting first and come back to account expansion later.

Desperately Seeking Value

When a buyer is having her first interaction with a new salesperson, the primary question in her mind is whether the salesperson and his company can offer her more value than her existing approach. Typically, the salesperson does the following:

- Explains what his company does

- Describes how his company's offering is different from that of the competition

- Tells stories about similar customers

- Asks for a follow-up discussion or a trial purchase

Better salespeople also demonstrate knowledge of the prospect's business, ask questions about her priorities, engage her in cocreating a solution, and demonstrate documented business results from other work. The best salespeople do all of the above, plus they tailor every interaction to only focus on the things that are the most important to the customer. Two outcomes typically result from these conversations:

1. **She's just not that into you.** Sometimes the prospect essentially throws the salesperson out the door because she's just not interested. Often she's happy with her current provider. Sometimes the particular offering the salesperson is selling is not high enough on her priority list to spend time on. In that case, she may refer the salesperson to someone else on her team. Or she may just say some variation of "This is really interesting. Now is not the right time, but I appreciate your coming by today, and I'll keep you in mind for when we're ready to consider this." It's the equivalent of "Don't call us, we'll call you."

2. **Risky business.** Often, the best achievable outcome is the prospect offering to explore the possibility further. In these situations, the prospect is now considering taking on a considerable amount of risk in trying something new

in exchange for a hope of better rewards in the future. Her willingness to take on the risk depends a lot on how successfully the salesperson painted a highly attractive but believable vision of the alternative future.

In the first scenario, the prospect dismissed the option of taking on the risk of a new solution, at least for the time being. In the second option, she began to take on some risk and to explore taking on more risk. The question for salespeople is, How can you encourage prospects to take the second option and to accelerate their exploration (or buying) process?

Risk Management

So we have a client who is, in her head, calculating risk and assessing whether to explore an approach that is different from what she has done in the past. As mentioned earlier, one strategy to increase her openness to this exploration is to increase the potential reward by depicting an attractive but realistic vision of what a better future could be. We will explore techniques to do this further in Chapter 14.

The other strategy for salespeople is to minimize the risk. There are two traditional ways to do this, and we're going to offer a powerful third way.

- **Reduce the real risk**. Offer trials. Invite the customer to a "customer experience center" to see the solution in action. Offer a significant discount on the first purchase. Structure the pricing so that the customer only pays for what is used without a large up-front commitment. Provide service-level guarantees.

- **Reduce the perception of risk.** Provide references of other happy customers. Help the prospect understand that the likelihood of problems is minimal. Tell stories of successful implementations. Address explicit and implicit concerns. Chapter 13 will offer 10 compelling ways to reduce the perception of risk.

Now here's the third way:

- **Serve before you sell.** Give the prospect something of value before she buys anything. By providing value, you will shift the way she perceives you and encourage reciprocal behavior.

What It Looks Like to Serve

Let's look more closely at what it means to serve before you sell. First, let's be clear on what serving is not. Serving is not about bringing doughnuts, key chains, thumb drives, or pens to your customer. It's not about sponsoring a pizza lunch for the customer's office. It's not about offering gifts or presents. Gift giving is a perfectly legitimate thing, particularly when used to genuinely express thanks or to show people that you care about them. But serving is different from gift giving.

Serving is about fulfilling a specific need or priority you've identified in your conversations with a customer or prospect. When you serve someone, it always involves doing something specific and customized for that individual. That is, it's not something you do for a group of similar people. It's not about adding people to mass e-mail lists or newsletters in hope that they might find something useful there. It has to be for an individual, and it has to be in direct response to a need or priority that individual has.

Identifying the need or priority is part of the magic. In a prospecting conversation with a prospect, you might hear any number of things with which you can help, even without the prospect buying anything. Here are examples of customer cues that trigger ways to serve the customer:

- The customer confesses a major challenge that she doesn't know how to address. You might serve her by providing an article or blog post of which she was unaware that addresses exactly that issue.

- You discover that the customer is struggling with a particular element of his operations, where your company has great expertise. You offer to connect him with your own internal experts.

- Your customer has a large multisite organization where communication with headquarters is weak. Use your local account managers to help drive communication in both directions.

- Your customer is preparing for a critical meeting with her executives, and you offer to help prepare a slide for a presentation.

- The customer might disclose that he is looking to hire someone with a specific background, and you provide the name of a LinkedIn group that would be a great place to post a job listing.

- The customer may mention that she is spending her vacation fly-fishing in Montana, and you know an expert on fly-fishing in Montana. Or a great place to eat . . . or to fish.

You can serve your customers' personal or professional needs or priorities. It doesn't matter. What does matter is that it's about the customers and what they are looking for, not about you (see Figure 12.4).

Opportunities to Serve

- Challenges
- Aspirations
- Innovations
- Gap analysis
- Stakeholder management
- Presentations
- Meeting facilitation
- Finding job candidates
- Personal goals
- Vacations and travel
- Family and children

Ways to Serve

- Books
- Articles, blog posts, tweets
- Connecting people
- Free advice or consulting
- Assistance with preparing documents or presentations
- Websites, LinkedIn groups
- Dining and travel recommendations

Figure 12.4   How to serve a prospect.

Social science research has shown that gifts are most likely to result in reciprocal behavior when the favors are *unexpected* and *personalized*. That's why figuring out what your customers' needs and priorities are is the first step. And the second step is giving them something they wouldn't have expected from a salesperson or don't get from other salespeople who call on them.

Why Serving Works

Why does it work to serve your customers first before selling? And does it really lead to a sale?

There are two powerful reasons why serving can be so useful in selling.

Sparking the Value Exchange

First, one of the hardest parts of prospecting is getting new customers to engage in a value exchange with you. They might meet with you and even listen to you, but will they take the next step into a business transaction? When you offer value first, instead of requiring them to agree to a purchase first, you make it easier to establish that business relationship.

In a normal selling situation, the business relationship truly begins when the customer either signs a contract or agrees to an initial purchase. In those situations, the customer is the first one to put real value on the table. By serving the customer first, the salesperson is putting value on the table. That makes it easier for the customer to move to the next step.

Wait, though. You might say that throughout a sales process, the salesperson is offering all sorts of value: information about solutions, options and alternatives, reference cases, etc. But rarely are these differentiated. Every supplier offers some version of the same thing. The key in serving the customer first is to do it in a differentiated way. This typically comes down to the salesperson more than the selling company. Great salespeople are always finding ways to serve the particular needs of their individual prospects and customers. It's part of what makes customers loyal to them. They do it in a way that is unique to them, because of their personal interests, connections, passion, and resources.

Triggering Reciprocity

Second, people are naturally wired to be reciprocal. All human societies require reciprocal behavior. We are brought up to repay people for their kindness. This social web of indebtedness, where people share food and skills, is deeply rooted in evolution. In fact, we consider it antisocial to violate reciprocity rules, and we apply derisive labels to people who do, such as "freeloader," "moocher," "parasite," "ingrate," etc. People go to great lengths to avoid being considered ungrateful. Not responding to a favor produces both internal discomfort and external shame.

In *Go Wild*, Harvard Medical School professor John Ratey, MD, and journalist Richard Manning explore the evolutionary basis of many of our behaviors, including this reciprocity obligation. They describe the biochemistry of community and the role that the hormone oxytocin plays in our desire to be altruistic, which enables our society to function. For a moment their research turns to the business world:

> Research has also shown that oxytocin plays a key role in business transactions, especially in establishing trust. This is not as squishy as it might sound. Economists will tell you that the workings of the

marketplace depend on a foundation of trust, that the glue of our economic lives rests on our ability to trust one another well enough to do deals.

The authors go on to say:

> People engaged in business transactions produce a spurt of oxytocin. If one person gives another person ten dollars, the recipient's oxytocin levels spike a bit. But here's the kicker: if a computer gives that same person ten dollars, his levels of oxytocin do not increase.

A corollary of the reciprocity obligation happens all the time during negotiations. There is a social obligation to make concessions to those who have made concessions to us. Used thoughtfully and strategically, this approach to concessions can kick-start a stalled negotiation.

Remember, though, that for reciprocity obligations to be triggered, the act of serving has to be noble and unconditional. You do not serve customers because you are expecting them to buy something from you as a direct result. You serve them because you can and because it is the right thing to do. If you become manipulative with how you serve people, people will see through it, and it will not work.

Account Expansion

For simplicity, the examples above focus on prospecting. But do the same tactics work with existing customers? Yes. Finding people's interests and needs and serving them by providing something unexpected and personalized always works. But you have to do it early in your relationship. Once the buyer questions your value, it can be too late to change that person's mind.

With more and more of today's buying processes turning into multiplayer games, we see salespeople forgetting to manage all the stakeholders. One way to address the multiple players now engaged in each buying decision is to identify their interests and needs and provide them with something unexpected and personalized.

Listeners Wanted

We live in a world today where almost every moment is filled with e-mails, tweets, news feed updates, mobile phone alerts, and text messages. We're bombarded with updates, but most have limited value to us. We're surprised and gratified, then, when something personalized and useful comes our way.

Perhaps the most important element of serving customers is that it shows you have listened. You have listened to what is uniquely relevant to them. That act overcomes a tremendous hurdle with prospects and customers who report that salespeople typically do not listen. By establishing that you are a listener, you change the game and become a welcome partner to that prospect or customer.

Conclusion—Driving the Customer Along the X → XY → Y Path

This chapter has articulated the specific behaviors that enable salespeople to sell in a way that accelerates their customers' desired business results. Each of these behaviors contributes to your ability to help your customers get to their intended destination. Let's take a quick look at how each of the behaviors mentioned enables the salesperson to help customers get to their desired Y faster.

In moving customers on the $X \rightarrow XY \rightarrow Y$ path, deep knowledge of each customer's business and industry allows a richer conversation and therefore one that can be had with executive decision makers. Because the $X \rightarrow XY \rightarrow Y$ journey is new, planning before each customer interaction is vital. These are complicated conversations. Using discovery skills to ask intelligent and provocative questions creates an interactive atmosphere in which alternative scenarios can be explored.

By engaging customers in cocreating the offering you will sell to them, you become their partner, and you shape a proposal that acknowledges their position on their $X \rightarrow XY \rightarrow Y$ journey. It will be hard for a competitor to do that. By understanding their decision-making process in the context of their journey (and the decision vortices that will inevitably slow decisions down), you can help them make smarter choices faster, advancing their purchasing decisions. When you take a view of your portfolio of customers that strategically identifies where they are on their X-to-Y journey, you can better prioritize your limited time. Working with others in your organization, you can collaborate in ways that bring unexpected expertise to your customers as they move through their change process.

If you are the key account manager, it becomes critical not only to understand your customers' business but also to know how their business drivers are changing. When you work with just one customer organization, you have to have an even deeper level of insight into that customer's world. Additionally, you must be able to create business cases quickly, both so that you can prepare them on the spot in front of customers and so that you can present them internally in your own company on your customers' behalf. With change occurring rapidly, you must be able to defend the value of your offerings on the spot in the face of new customer priorities and access additional company resources quickly.

If you are prospecting, you want to serve before you sell. You can spark a value exchange and trigger reciprocity by providing your prospect or customer with articles, connections, advice, and assistance in defining Y or XY or making the X → XY → Y journey. Simply by describing how an X → XY → Y approach can make a change initiative more successful will in itself be of tremendous service.

CHAPTER 13

Great Selling: Addressing Buying Delays

I n Chapters 8 and 9, we looked at how change efforts are, perhaps counterintuitively, actually slowing down customer buying decisions. Risk avoidance is becoming a priority for those who work in a climate of fear and uncertainty. Additionally, when strategic initiatives are paused for reconsideration, there is a cascading effect throughout the organization that can halt purchasing decisions. The good news is that the right set of salesperson behaviors can help minimize or eliminate these delays.

Decision Vortices

Viewing the x-ray of corporate decision making that comes from understanding decision vortices (Chapter 9) suggests a number of lessons for salespeople who manage major sales.

Lesson #1: It's Not About You

We can't count the number of stories we have heard where a customer is about to make a major purchase and the salesperson has already calculated his commission and spent it in his head, only to find that the purchase has been delayed due to a decision vortex in a related strategic initiative. At times like this, some sales forces offer the customer a new deal, hoping to accelerate the purchase decision. Big discounts are offered, particularly near the end of a quarter. But it doesn't matter, because the delay is not driven by concerns about price. It is driven by a larger decision vortex connected to the overall strategic initiative. Offering a pricing incentive will not speed up the decision; it will just telegraph to the customer that you were charging too much to begin with.

Purchasing delays caused by decision vortices aren't "objections" in the traditional sense. The delays are indicators that the customer is figuring out how to manage the larger initiative. The only way to win in these situations is to stay focused on advancing the customer's buying process, not your sales process. The lessons that follow describe how to do that.

Lesson #2: Apply Navigation Skills

The best sellers are willing to sacrifice today's opportunity and offer their best advice to the client. Using the expertise they've gained from working with similar companies in similar situations and using their understanding of the ultimate results the customer is trying to achieve, they offer options—paths—the customer can use to get to the desired destination.

Using navigation skills (which were described in Chapter 11) means:

- **Clarifying the destination.** You can't be an advisor to your customers unless you understand their vision of success, their goals, and the metrics they use to measure progress on those goals. From time to time, in the process of executing, people lose track of their goals. It's the salesperson's role to re-anchor the customer on the desired destination. Salespeople with navigation skills get a seat at the table because they are destination experts, almost like travel agents who specialize, for example, in African safaris, European river cruises, or whitewater rafting experiences.

- **Recommending the path.** Salespeople who use navigation skills provide insights. Challenging traditional thinking and insight selling are concepts we have been championing since 2006, when McGraw-Hill published our book *The Mind of the Customer*. But with all the talk today about insight selling, much is getting lost in the noise. Relevant insights come from personal experience working with similar customers trying to do similar things. Just like a backwoods hiking navigator, the salesperson has to know the options, the shortcuts, and the hazards to avoid. The easiest way for a salesperson to share this knowledge is to (1) understand current marketplace trends and discuss the likelihood and severity of their potential impacts on this company and (2) provide three realistic options, or execution paths, and the advantages and disadvantages of each.

- **Measuring progress.** Navigator salespeople assume a role in benchmarking the progress that the customer organization is achieving on its metrics. The best of these salespeople play this role even if they don't have a current sales cycle in play.

Without disclosing any nonpublic proprietary information, they aggregate the data they have from other organizations and point out where their customer is succeeding and where the gaps are.

Lesson #3: Swift-Water Rescue: Get the Customer Out of the Vortex

Can a salesperson really move a customer out of a decision vortex? Yes. The vortex is driven by uncertainty and fear. The seller can be an objective listener to those concerns and address them rationally.

Rarely is the salesperson able to join the executive meetings where risk and uncertainty are discussed. But what they are able to do is to speak to a number of C-suite stakeholders before and after those meetings. It is in those discussions that the salesperson needs to offer an objective analysis of risks and options, giving each stakeholder essentially a set of talking points to bring into the meeting.

Helping a customer out of a decision vortex means recognizing that the decision vortex is at its heart a prioritization exercise. People are reevaluating the priority of competing initiatives and competing projects and purchases within each initiative. The salesperson needs to provide tools and insights (as described above) to help them make those decisions.

Prioritization discussions often come down to conversations about:

- Cost containment

- Risk reduction

- Revenue growth

- Asset utilization

- Customer experience

- Product launches

- Employee engagement

The salesperson must be able to have stakeholder conversations about each of those objectives, doing it in the context of the full strategic initiative, not just in the context of what the salesperson is selling, though that is important too, of course.

There is an old saying, "When in doubt, do nothing." That is probably terrible advice in many situations, but it does describe what happens in a lot of executive suites these days. So it is the salesperson's job to reduce or eliminate the doubt. That means:

- Demonstrating the cost (in additional expense, lost revenue, time) from the delay.

- Offering insights about best practices in these situations. These insights are most applicable when they are specific to the customer's industry and specific to each stakeholder's functional responsibilities.

- Breaking the initiative into smaller, more manageable chunks. Describing an X → XY → Y approach can provide great value.

- Helping customers make connections within their own organization. Many account managers have cross-functional insights that enable leaders to see beyond their silos.

In summary, the best time to do insight selling is often when a customer is in a reevaluation vortex. Where executives need help is in figuring out the right timing for different investments. Insights about the best timing and sequence for those investments will have the most value.

Lesson #4: Connect to Multiple Initiatives

There's a long body of work in investment research that says no one can pick a single stock investment successfully. That's why mutual funds or portfolios are what make sense for the average investor. The same is true for strategic initiatives. The more initiatives your sale is connected to, the more diversified you are.

Think about the four strategic initiatives we illustrated in Chapter 9. If your sale is only connected to Strategic Initiative #2, and that is the one the customer stops, then you're in trouble. But even if you've been brought in to help with Strategic Initiative #2, you can ask questions about the other initiatives and create linkages between what you sell and the other initiatives. That is insurance. Through your questions, you may be able to figure out that Strategic Initiative #4 is the CEO's personal priority and key to achieving the company's goals. Make sure you create a legitimate connection between what you sell and that one. Remember, it all has to be in the context of the business results the customer is trying to achieve.

Another way that accelerator salespeople use navigator skills to provide advice to customers is by helping them see hidden connections between initiatives. For instance, Strategic Initiative #1 may be about revenue growth, and Strategic Initiative #4 may be about consolidating manufacturing facilities. Sounds disconnected, right? But what if buried in the factory consolidation initiative is a plan to increase production in Mexico? How can that investment be leveraged to broaden sales activity and distribution channels in the Mexican market?

The more detail you know about the underlying elements of each strategic initiative, the more credible and useful suggestions you can make about how to execute the initiatives more effectively.

Lesson #5: Reduce Individual Risk

Organizations go into a decision vortex for a reason. The rate of change has increased to the point that even very capable people no longer trust their own judgment. This creates an environment where many members of a buying committee can veto anything with their vote but approve nothing on their own. There is significant risk for an individual to stand out from the others and push for resolution. The best sellers respect the individual challenges of each stakeholder while finding ways to reduce this risk and help key stakeholders develop the tools to pull their peers from the vortex.

Buyer Inaction

An additional set of lessons can be applied to address a stalled buying process when the cause is not a strategic initiative but rather buyer inaction, as described in Chapter 8.

Lesson #6: Emphasize Potential Losses from Inaction

"Moving people under conditions of uncertainty is difficult—the first thing they do is freeze. They're scared of what they might lose. Therefore it's good to tell people what they will lose if they *fail* to move." That's a quote from Robert Cialdini, a leading social scientist and the author of the book *Influence*, from an interview in the *Harvard Business Review*. He continues, "Notions of loss are psychologically more powerful than notions of gain."

That idea was proved in a series of experiments that helped the psychologist Daniel Kahneman win the Nobel Prize in Economics. In one example, Kahneman gave a choice to his three separate classes. In Class A, students could choose between a mug with their university logo on it or some Swiss chocolate. Fifty-nine percent chose the mug, which suggests the mug had a slightly higher value. In Class B, students were given the mug at the outset and offered the chance to trade it for the chocolate. Eighty-nine percent kept the mug. In Class C, students were given the chocolate and then asked if they wanted to trade it for the mug. Only 10 percent were willing to make the trade. The experiment shows that people put more value on a good that they already own than on a good that they do not own, regardless of value. This phenomenon is why home sellers always think their houses are worth more than buyers do.

A similar experiment showed that students who were loss avoiders had an even more pronounced aversion to giving up what they had (not surprisingly). But gain maximizers also avoided giving up what they had, even more so if they were instructed to think about *what they would gain by keeping what they had* (as opposed to focusing *on what they would lose* by giving something up).

Chapter 10 explained how the world of sales has shifted. Customers today are not looking for salespeople who can fill their needs for *products*. Nor are they looking for salespeople who can create *solutions* to their problems. They want salespeople to help *accelerate their desired business results*. Combine that with Cialdini's advice and Kahneman's experiments, and what you get is this: salespeople dealing with customers struggling with an uncertain environment must make sure the customers understand that their business goals are at risk if they do not act. For loss avoiders, it's easy to frame this message: explain the risks. For gain maximizers, emphasize the goals they can achieve by acting.

Let's be clear. This is not the old solution-selling approach of finding a problem in a business process and increasing the pain attached to that problem. *Building the pain* or focusing on negative *implications* beyond the customer's reality is a very dangerous game to play. Today's savvy buyers will quickly eliminate sellers who are seen as manipulative. It's about making the impact of inaction on overall business results explicit.

Consider the following:

- Can your customer achieve the desired business results without taking action?

- What target metrics are at risk if the company fails to act?

- Can a compelling story be told about what might happen through inaction?

- Which of the company's strategic initiatives might be at risk if action is not taken?

- When must action be taken before it is too late? What are the contingency plans?

In times of uncertainty, people are obsessed with the illusion that doing nothing is safer than taking action. Because buyers appreciate honest and direct dialogue about their current business realities, you can create tremendous value and accelerate the buying cycle by framing inactivity as a significant barrier to achieving their business results.

Lesson #7: Bring in the Experts

Cialdini also mentions that in times of uncertainty, people "don't look inside themselves for answers—all they see is ambiguity and their own lack of confidence. Instead, they look outside for sources of information that can reduce their uncertainty. The first thing they look to is authority: What do the experts think about this topic?" That means the salesperson must do one or more of three things:

1. **Be the expert that customers seek.** Demonstrate an understanding of the customer's industry and business. Clarify the results the customer seeks. Recommend a path. Measure progress.

2. **Bring experts to the table.** Leverage others in your organization who have expertise. Arrange for them to talk to your customers.

3. **Demonstrate what well-respected experts think.** Provide articles, reports, and white papers that define the state-of-the-art and, in particular, the costs of inaction (for loss preventers) or the potential gains from action (for gain maximizers).

Of course, when delivering expertise, it is important to acknowledge the experience of your buyers and the reality that you could never understand the specific details of their circumstances. Behaving with respect and humility makes the difference between being arrogant and being insightful.

Lesson #8: Recognize the Power of Social Pressure

While people consistently look to experts during periods of uncertainty, they also look to peers. In fact, in our socially networked world of today, peer influence may be overtaking expert influence. Think about your own purchases. You're probably more likely to be influenced by what a friend posts about a restaurant or a book than what a review says.

This idea is backed up by recent behavioral research. A study of lifeguards in Australia shows that lifeguards are more likely to practice safe sun protection habits if they think their peers are applying those same practices.

A fascinating experiment run by Cialdini and several colleagues illustrates the power of peers and social influence in decision making. The experiment focused on reusing towels in hotels. The team created two cards for placement in hotel rooms. One card had the basic environmental protection message that we're all familiar with; the second informed guests that the majority of guests at the hotel reused their towels at least once during their

stay. Those guests who got the second social message were 26 percent more likely than those who saw the basic environmental protection message to reuse their towels. In a follow-up study, if the
guest's card said that the majority of people who stayed *in that
particular room* reused their towels, towel reuse increased to 33
percent above what the basic environmental message achieved.

How can you apply this to your customers who are slow
about making buying decisions?

1. Help benchmark the customers against their peers. Define
   what "great" looks like in their industry or their functional
   area by documenting what the best companies are doing.
   Then help the customers rate themselves on how they
   compare with those leaders.

2. Make sure your slow-decision buyers are aware of how
   other buyers in their organization (and perhaps even in
   other companies) are moving forward with their buying
   decisions on the items you sell to them.

3. Acknowledge that the buying-decision process takes
   longer today and that each buyer's company is "special
   and unique." But also provide some data on how long the
   buying process typically lasts at your other customers.

Here's some advice on how peer pressure works differently
with loss preventers and gain maximizers. Loss preventers are
highly attuned to people inside their group or organization. They
will tend to tune out people from the outside as not understanding or not being relevant to their world or situation. (They tend
to view outsiders as risky.) Research by Heidi Grant Halvorson
and Tory Higgins suggests that gain maximizers are neutral to

outsiders, but our own experience says that gain maximizers have great appreciation for outsiders who bring new insights or new opportunities to help accomplish their goals.

Lesson #9: Manage the Stakeholders

Could it be that an increased reliance on peers is also slowing down decision making? More stakeholders at the table create slower decisions? Well, it's probably true.

When risk avoidance takes over as the dominant culture, people involve more stakeholders in each decision. Because so many people have lost their jobs over the last few years, many employees don't want to put their own jobs at risk. So before making big decisions, they consult others, giving themselves protection if the decision goes wrong. That means that a lot of people have to be consulted before a decision is made. They are afraid to execute in a way that could be criticized down the road, so they only move forward on projects where the stakeholders are in consensus.

Oftentimes any one stakeholder can say "no" or "not now," but it takes almost everyone to agree to create a "yes." That means fewer yeses and more delays as decisions move through the stakeholder deliberation process. It also means projects and purchases can stall when a buyer hasn't received sufficient internal support to move forward but believes in the project enough that he is unwilling to let the idea die. That can result in a familiar situation where a sale sits in the funnel forever, with the client saying he's not quite ready yet and the salesperson being understandably reluctant to show the deal as a loss (particularly since it hasn't been awarded to a competitor), but there is no forward progress in the sales cycle either.

As we mentioned in Chapter 4, buyers today take economic, technical, and user considerations into account simultaneously. It's no longer useful to assume that different people have responsibility for each of these considerations. It also seems that labeling stakeholders as "supporters," "advocates," "champions," or "coaches," on the one hand, or as "opponents" or "blockers," on the other, is actually counterproductive. Seeing customer stakeholders as friends or enemies is too black or white. It encourages a strategy of leveraging supporters and minimizing the concerns of opponents. That might work well in election campaigns, where the game is zero sum, but it doesn't work in sales. All people have interests they are trying to pursue. Some of those interests are aligned with your proposal in an obvious way; some are more subtle. By understanding the interests of those stakeholders who are not yet supportive of your proposal, you will likely find ways to address what is important to them. If you write them off as enemies, you'll never get the chance.

In any case, you want to identify the dominant focus (gain maximizer or loss avoider) for each stakeholder and be sure to speak his language.

Lesson #10: Keep the Choices Simple

When buyers respond to organizational turbulence with risk-avoidance behaviors, is it better to provide customers with more choices—or fewer?

Behavioral scientists Sheena Iyengar and Mark Lepper ran an experiment in a supermarket, offering free samples of jam while monitoring the jam purchases of those who tried the samples. When 6 flavors of jam were put out for sampling, 30 percent of the samplers purchased jam. But when 24 flavors were provided as samples, only 3 percent made a jam purchase. When too many choices are available, people consistently choose the current state. Professor Iyengar said, "In reality, people might find more and more choice to actually be debilitating."

This is particularly true in times of uncertainty. Already burdened by the cognitive processing required by the state of change, people act to reduce the number of decisions that need to be made. When customers are already uncertain about their purchase requirements, having too many choices can drive them to continue the status quo.

Compounding that problem is the way many salespeople present proposals. First, there are too many options and alternatives. It's easy to think that options and alternatives give customers flexibility to create the solution they really need. But the truth is that you're putting customers in front of one of those custom salad bars, where there are 75 ingredients and they can have almost whatever they want. That setup is great if you know exactly what you want, if, say, you go there every week. But if it's the first time or it has been a while, it's overwhelming—and much easier to take one of the premade salads sitting nearby. Give people too many choices or decisions to make, and you can be pretty certain that they will do nothing.

Second, many proposals make it hard for the customer to understand the pricing. The options and alternatives above play into this complexity. But even with simple solutions, it's common to see pricing broken down in ways that match the seller's cost structure (e.g., fixed- and variable-cost items priced separately) that don't at all match the way the customer thinks of budgeting, spending, or investing. If you ever need a quick reminder of this challenge, just review the room service menu at a hotel. You have to pay for the items you order, plus a service charge or gratuity, plus a "delivery charge." That fits the hotel's cost structure. But it makes it really hard to figure out how much a couple of eggs and a coffee will actually cost you.

If you want your customers to make buying decisions despite uncertainty, keep their choices simple.

Gain maximizers thrive on having alternatives, so give them some, but keep them simple. Loss preventers are more concerned about analyzing alternatives. They want a matrix where they can compare individual components of each alternative, rather than the option as a whole (which is the way gain maximizers look at things). Make sure you accommodate both approaches in your proposals, and keep them simple and clear.

Conclusion—The Rewards of Reducing Uncertainty

David Rock, head of the NeuroLeadership Institute, is a researcher who has synthesized current neuroscience research on how people interact socially. One of Rock's conclusions is that the brain is constantly trying to predict the near future. Since the brain is a pattern-recognition machine, it craves certainty, so that prediction is possible. Without prediction, the brain must use dramatically more resources, involving the more energy-intensive prefrontal cortex, to process moment-to-moment experience.

Rock told the *New York Times*:

> Uncertainty feels like pain. When you're holding multiple possible futures in your head, that turns out to

be cognitively exhausting. And the more we can predict the future, the more rewarded we feel. The less we can predict the future, the more threatened we feel. As soon as any ambiguity arises in even a very simple activity, we get a threat response. So we are driven to create certainty.

Small uncertainties make it difficult to focus, and large uncertainties can be debilitating. Conversely, feeling more certain about things is rewarding, and feeling that expectations are being met releases dopamine—the reward-response neurotransmitter—in the brain. Once the brain is back in a situation where it has available mental maps, it feels better.

We live in an increasingly uncertain world, but uncertainty can be decreased. Plans drive clarity about the future, or at least about likely futures. Simplifying complicated projects into smaller chunks has the same effect, reducing that overwhelming feeling that comes from not having mental maps already in place. Talking about possible future situations, or scenario planning, is also effective.

Think of the X → XY → Y approach as a road map that can become a mental model for your customers, providing clarity and reducing uncertainty. That will not only help them execute more efficiently and successfully; it will also reduce decision delays that prevent them from making a purchase with you.

PART 4

Sales Managers and Sales Leaders: Changing Selling

CHAPTER 14

Great Sales Management: Leading People

S omehow, over the last two decades, conventional wisdom has locked into a singular view of the role of sales managers. The notion is that the primary role of the sales manager is to coach salespeople. This is ironic because, in our experience working with 50 of the world's leading sales forces, none of them would report that their sales managers are doing an adequate job of coaching. Is having a universally accepted standard of the sales manager as a coach accurate or useful? Probably not.

In the next chapter we'll discuss why the whole notion of coaching is worth questioning. Here let's get a better picture of what great sales management looks like today. The easiest way to get a window into great sales management is to look at what happens when salespeople become sales managers for the first time. (It is easy here to repeat the other piece of related conventional wisdom: great salespeople often don't make great sales managers.

True. But the most logical place to look for new sales managers is always going to be from the existing pool of high-performing salespeople. You just have to select the ones with the right skills and personal attributes.)

Some successful salespeople, when appointed to their first sales management position, initially focus almost exclusively on customers. They spend a lot of time going on sales calls with their team. They remove roadblocks that are getting in the way of closing deals. In some cases, they continue to manage opportunities or relationships. Overall, they believe their path to success as a sales manager is to be what we call "customer advocates."

Other newly promoted sales managers find it difficult to shift from being a peer to their team to their boss. They become the "buddy" sales manager, always willing to step in and help, whatever is needed. In the better versions of this approach, they focus their energy on developing their team members, believing that the greatest success will come from everyone working at his or her potential.

The third situation happens when new sales managers actually develop an affinity for all those reports they are now required to produce for their company. They become a bit of a spreadsheet jockey, constantly moving numbers around to get the reports right. They are not as available to their team or customers, but their bosses sure appreciate being able to get quick data. We call these sales managers, "administrators."

Which of these three options is the best approach? None of them and all of them. That is, successful sales managers have to balance their focus on all three of these areas—customer, team, and company—all at once (see Figure 14.1). When they overfocus on one area, another suffers. The question that sales

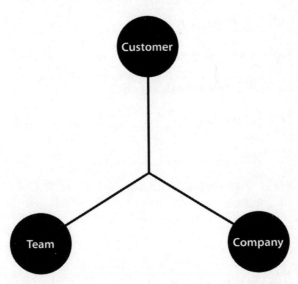

Figure 14.1   Three areas of potential focus for sales managers.

managers should ask themselves every day is, "Am I balancing my time across the needs of our customers, the needs of my team, and the needs of my company?"

Even with a balanced approach, the life of a sales manager is difficult. We might even say impossible. We believe there is a major restructuring of sales management coming around the corner. Sales managers are expected to do far too much. Take a look at what most companies hope sales managers will do:

- Set expectations.

- Observe customer meetings and coach before and after.

- Provide in-the-moment feedback during planning and office activities.

- Set development priorities.

- Embed classroom training.

- Interview and select new salespeople.

- Manage the job candidate pipeline.

- Oversee onboarding.

- Sell.

- Maintain relationships with key customers.

- Plan.

- Report.

- Manage the sales pipeline.

There is not enough time in a day, a week, or a quarter to do a good job on all these activities. Moreover, this list doesn't include a host of activities that we have found are necessary for high-performing sales managers. We'll describe those later in this chapter and in the two subsequent chapters.

As a result of having too many activities, most sales managers focus on a few where they are strong while doing the best job they can on a set of secondary priorities, and usually leaving out altogether a few activities on the list above.

Here are some of the changes we see coming to the way sales management is organized:

- Some development of salespeople will move to field coaches who have this as their primary responsibility. These field coaches become experts both in the desired skills and in the process of behavioral change. Companies that already apply this approach find it powerful. The risk, however, which we have seen several times, is that after a couple of bad quarters, these positions are the first to be eliminated, along with all people development activities, like training. Good leaders have to see these positions as long-term investments. To link the positions more directly to their revenue contribution, leaders can structure compensation incentives that are driven in part by how much revenue increases among the people being coached.

- Technology will replace some sales management activities. A significant portion of the sales manager's job involves communication and development. Increasingly, technology can perform large portions of that work more efficiently. From a distance, this can look like the predictions of the 1950s where kitchen and laundry technology promised homemakers a life of leisure. That's not exactly the case. However, technology can provide new and relevant information to salespeople on a daily basis, analyze data to recommend customer and development priorities, deliver short learning solutions, and provide feedback based on CRM data. Videos can show what "great" looks like, and social features can allow salespeople to learn from their peers. Technology to do all these things already exists.

In thinking about what the sales manager of the future looks like, we have found the most useful model to be one that breaks the job into three components:

- Leading people

- Developing people

- Executing the plan

In the remainder of this chapter, we will outline the key activities required to successfully lead people and describe what is particularly critical during periods of X-to-Y change. The other two components, developing people and executing the plan, will be discussed in the chapters that follow.

Communicate Vision

When it comes to the manager's role in leading people, the standard view is that the most important focus for the leader is setting expectations. That is true, but we find that it is incomplete. Salespeople want to know more than just what is expected of them. They want to know why. Particularly among the increasing number of millennial salespeople, there is also a desire to be connected to and contributing to a larger purpose. The best sales managers today—the ones that sales reps remember for the rest of their career—are those who inspire people with a larger sense of purpose, based on the mission, vision, and values of the company. Of course, their success also comes from focusing on achievement of quantitative targets, but they don't focus only on the numbers.

Great sales managers today understand that they must have a vision for their team. Yes, there might be an overall corporate vision, but they also create one that is aligned to the larger vision but shows what success will be for their sales team. They share that vision directly and through stories and examples of how people are contributing to the vision's attainment.

These great sales managers also show how each person's plan is aligned with the company's strategy and plan for the current performance year. When times get tough—which they almost inevitably do at some point—these managers motivate their team by focusing on the bigger picture and offering a longer-term view that shows how things will get better.

It's probably not hard to see how the ability to communicate a vision becomes a vital element of success in a world of X-to-Y change. First, the manager has to explain what Y is, what it means, and why it is vital for the company's and the salespeople's future. To be successful, this must be done with authenticity; that is, sales managers need to speak from the heart about why they think this is the right thing to do.

Second, sales managers have to articulate what a Y future looks like for their teams, not just for the company as a whole. Next, and this is the most important part and the theme of this book, managers have to describe the shorter-term XY picture of success. They have to communicate to salespeople how X and Y will be sold at the same time to the same customers. An essential part of this work is emphasizing that X business and the people who sell X are still highly valued. Managers have to explain the new measures of success, which must contain metrics for X, XY, and Y.

Demonstrate Executive Presence

Increasingly, the sales leaders we work with at the world's largest sales forces expect their sales managers to show up internally and externally as executives would. That means that when working with their teams, sales managers cannot express cynicism about new policies or strategies. They can't blame leaders for wrong-headed moves. They have to own the company strategy as if it were their own. That means they cannot remain neutral either. Sales managers who demonstrate executive presence are no longer just messengers of news from above. They are partners in executing the strategy. Sales managers who have figured all this out also have discovered another secret: this approach is also the fast path to promotion.

Whether they appreciate it or not, sales managers are always "on stage" with their team. Their people are watching what they do and assessing whether they want to be led into battle by this person. That means that managers must act from authentic conviction. People will quickly spot anything less than full honesty. So that means that, prior to talking to their teams, sales managers have to genuinely align their mindset with the new strategy, change, or policy announcement.

In a world of X-to-Y change, the ability of sales managers to demonstrate executive presence will surely be tested. Not only must they communicate the vision, as we described earlier. They must do it with authentic conviction. They must go through their own change journey to develop comfort with the new approach before explaining it to their teams. They have to own it.

Behaving as an executive also contains an external component. The sales manager is often the leadership face of the company to customers and the local community. That means the manager has to be able to articulate the company's strategy to customers in a way that is relevant to them and to what their own businesses are trying to accomplish. Sales managers have to behave, dress, and communicate in a manner that is consistent with their companies' values and brand.

During an X-to-Y change initiative, it falls upon sales managers to explain their companies' new approaches to customers. Telling this story is much simpler when the X → XY → Y approach is used. It's critical to define the company's Y future and how that intersects with the customer's future vision. Yet it's equally important to describe the XY midpoint and the company's commitment to continuing to sell X. What the XY midpoint looks like may vary for every customer. That must be co-created with each account. It's the sales manager's job to help assuage concerns and demonstrate that the X → XY → Y transition will be executed in full partnership with each customer.

Sales managers also must become internal role models for the company's values. They have to live those values as examples for others. That sounds easy, but the moments of truth are when they must make a decision where the interests of their own team conflict with those of another department. At moments like these, people are watching to see if the manager does the right thing for the company or the right thing for his own interests. Behaving as an executive means adopting a balanced approach, where the interests of the customer, the company, and the team are all considered.

Become the Voice of the Customer

While sales managers are not responsible for production or delivery, they are still on the line to make sure that customers are happy. For many sales managers, this means spending significant time addressing problems and acting as an ombudsperson for the customer with other company departments. Not only do the best sales managers do this, but they find the bigger patterns and prevent future problems by becoming the voice of the customer internally.

In the meetings they attend, these great sales managers remind people to consider the customers' point of view and how customers will be affected by big decisions. They do that at both the macro and micro level: How will our customers perceive us differently as a result of this announcement? How will a specific customer who is about to go out to bid on a big piece of business react? In the confusing mix of stakeholder discussions that most companies have, it is easy for the voice of the customer to get lost. The sales manager's job is to make sure that doesn't happen.

When companies are moving through an X → XY → Y change process, sales managers should ensure that customer needs and interests are protected. What will happen to customers who are still buying X? What does XY look like from the customers' point of view? How different might it look for different customers? What does achievement of Y mean for our current customer base? What new customers do we need to find? These questions should not be used to slow the transition down but rather to speed it up by providing the clarity that customers and salespeople will require.

Humility and Experimentation

Part of demonstrating integrity and authenticity is taking a humble approach to change. While the best leaders always have a vision and a plan, they also admit that they don't have everything figured out yet. It is better to admit that you believe the plan is 80 percent right and you'll figure out the rest along the way than it is to show an inflexible commitment to the perfection of a theoretical plan. By acknowledging that you will make adjustments along the way, you will show people that you will learn and adapt, which actually makes you more believable. The commitment to Y should never waver, but the exact path to Y will inevitably evolve over time.

One way to operationalize that approach is to experiment. You can try different approaches with different customers or different salespeople as you figure out what XY approach works best. These experiments work best when they are intentional and well communicated. Let people know they are experiments. Then collect data in as an objective way as possible. That will inform better decisions and build support for your XY implementation approach.

Conclusion—Value the Whole Journey

In a nutshell, sales managers must demonstrate (perhaps even more than anyone else in the business) that they authentically value X, XY, and Y. They cannot avoid Y (as many do) or fall in love with Y and neglect X (as some others do). On a day-to-day basis, they will benefit more than anyone else from having clarity about the XY midpoint. It will enable them to communicate better both upward to their leaders and downward to their teams, as well as to their customers.

CHAPTER 15

Great Sales Management: Developing People

S top for a moment and remember an early experience of doing something you had never done before. Remember the feeling of doing something you had really wanted to be great at as quickly as you could. Odds are it took someone who had been there before to help you understand the rules, avoid common mistakes, and make the most of your natural abilities. It doesn't matter whether your memory was from playing a sport, being on the debate team, or tying your shoes for the first time. The person who helped you was your coach.

The idea of using traditional coaching methods to help develop people on the job surged in popularity during the early 1990s. Over the last few decades, "coaching" has become both a signifier of the desirable way to manage people and a catchall term used haphazardly to group almost all manager-to-rep interactions. Most sales leaders (and virtually all sales training professionals) believe that if sales managers would just "coach" more frequently and effectively, then sales performance would improve.

The coaching that is used every day in sales organizations means conversations that involve some or all of the following:

- Encouraging self-discovery

- Assessing performance

- Providing feedback

- Setting goals

- Driving behavior change

- Having difficult conversations

- Building confidence

- Reinforcing training

Frequently the term "coaching" is employed when leaders want sales managers to change some aspect of salesperson behavior without coming across as being too directive or controlling. Their hope is that through some magic bag of coaching skills, the salesperson can be skillfully and subtly manipulated into discovering the new approach on his or her own. Occasionally that can work, but in our experience it's the exception, not the rule. Far more frequently, coaching conversations turn into a game where the salesperson knows exactly what the manager is trying to drive and just plays along.

The most frequent application of sales coaching follows a pattern:

1. The manager accompanies the salesperson to a visit with a customer (or listens in on a call).

2. Sometimes the manager has an observation checklist of behaviors to look for, but frequently does not.

3. After the customer interaction, the manager asks the rep to self-assess, "How do you think that went?"

4. The salesperson offers a few observations ("I could have done a better job of . . .") and then quickly shifts to discussing the customer or the opportunity.

5. The sales manager explains where he or she agrees and disagrees with the manager's self-assessment.

6. Together, the manager and rep agree on what the salesperson will do differently the next time.

7. In rare cases, the manager actually follows up afterward to ensure the committed actions are done.

Here are the problems with that approach. First, there are plenty of good models available for leading a traditional coaching interaction. However, few of them help managers diagnose the core issues, and even fewer drive the discipline required to form new habits. So coaching builds awareness of potential issues but not the pathways to results. Second, these conversations are only rarely guided by a larger development plan. In fact, from one coaching interaction to the next, it is likely the salesperson will be hearing about completely different areas to focus on. There is rarely any tieback to a previous conversation or a focus on one set of behaviors over a continuous period of time.

Theoretically, all these problems are fixable. A sales leader can emphasize and hold people accountable for taking coaching seriously, can ensure that coaching is linked to development plans, and can provide training that enables managers to coach effectively. In fact, many sales leaders have done exactly that, often involving great time and expense. And they still don't see the results they seek. Why not? The problem is this: sales managers just don't have time to coach with any frequency. Time for coaching isn't available. As we noted in the previous chapter, the list of responsibilities and activities for a sales manager today is impossibly long. Since coaching will never have the urgency that most other activities do, it always gets placed low on the list of priorities. Conceivably, a sales leader could reconfigure sales manager priorities, but except in a few cases where the entire company culture supports that focus on coaching and is willing to accept the trade-offs (particularly in the sales manager's role in reporting data), we have not seen that be successful.

The good news is that there are alternatives. As we mentioned in the last chapter, we believe that the whole sales management function will soon be restructured. It is too early to predict the outcome of that reconfiguration, but something will happen, and technology will likely play a role. Another option is an approach we will explore in a moment.

We have surveyed over 200 salespeople in different companies and asked them what types of experiences have had the biggest impact on their success. Coaching from sales managers does not rank at the top of the list of what impacts salesperson behavior. In fact the top impacts are from (1) feedback from customers, which is not surprising, (2) mentoring by a more experienced salesperson, and (3) feedback from peers, which brings us to our next point.

The Future of Coaching Begins to Emerge

Think about the kids you know that play sports. Most have a coach, right? Now think about the kids you know that play video games. How many of those have a coach? Probably zero. Why is that? We believe there are two reasons, and both offer lessons for the future of coaching in sales.

First, kids play video games together, with siblings or peers. They are watching what each other does to be successful. They learn from one another without consciously thinking about it. As the survey we mentioned above said, peer feedback is more effective in changing behavior than is feedback from a sales manager. As in video games, salespeople are watching their peers and seeing what makes people successful, and they are more open to suggestions from successful peers than to suggestions from their managers. Or they are more committed to making changes based on suggestions from peers than on suggestions from their manager. We believe that the future of sales coaching will involve significantly more mechanisms to encourage peer feedback. The incorporation of social media into corporations' internal communication systems is making this even easier.

Second, video games are built to provide constant behavioral feedback. You fail quickly in a video game, and even if the exact reason is not clear, you can engage in many cycles quickly to discover the reason (even in the absence of peers). We believe that future technology will bring ways of providing constant feedback to salespeople without the sales manager acting as an intermediary. A combination of improved data analytics (leveraging CRM data and other sources) will point out patterns that salespeople can use to make adjustments. We also believe that technology can replace or reduce many of the activities that sales managers must engage in today to develop salespeople. Among these are making video examples of "great" selling easily accessible, providing mechanisms for fast practice, helping to set development priorities, and guiding salespeople through self-assessments.

Demonstrating What "Great" Looks Like

We find that the term "coaching" is used so broadly today that it has ceased to be useful. In our own work, we try to avoid the term, and instead we drill deeper to get at what each sales leader is trying to drive. Is it feedback? Is it expectation setting? Performance management? Assessment? We then focus on exactly that need, rather than the generalized world of coaching. Often, the most critical assistance a sales manager can provide a seller is to demonstrate what "great" looks like. There are three ways a manager can offer this assistance.

Modeling

In today's world, people need to see what a behavior looks like in order to replicate it. You can tell them what is involved in, say, asking questions of a C-level executive, but most people need to see it in order to get it. The seller and the manager can agree before a call on what skills the manager will model and what the seller should expect to see. (See the next tip, "Co-Selling," for how to manage that customer meeting.) After the call, the seller should give the manager feedback and ask questions. The two can then have an open discussion about how the manager can be even better and how the salesperson can adopt the behaviors she saw. To some extent, modeling is the opposite of the salesperson practicing and receiving feedback.

Co-Selling

Here's another tip that contradicts conventional wisdom. It's widely believed that sales managers should play a passive, observational role when they accompany salespeople to a customer meeting. The fear is that the manager will "take over" the meeting. As a result, managers often sit relatively quietly. Yet salespeople actually learn best when they can watch someone demonstrate a new behavior. The answer to this dilemma is simple: managers and reps should decide before the meeting who will be responsible for each element of the conversation. The manager can take just one element of the meeting, such as asking discovery questions, whiteboarding a co-created solution, or advancing the customer to the next stage of the buying process. The remainder of the meeting can be led by the salesperson. The sales manager must, of course, refrain from taking over the sale.

This approach reinforces the idea of the salesperson and sales manager selling together, jointly responsible for the outcome of the meeting. It replaces the pressure of "being observed and judged" with a partnership in which both people are working together toward a collective goal. The follow-up discussion, after the meeting, can then delve into what was going on in each person's mind during the meeting. Sharing the underlying thought process is as important as getting the talk track right. After the meeting, there are typically further opportunities for the manager and salesperson to collaborate. They can work together on any deliverables where the salesperson is still developing capability.

Practice

Oddly, while the world of sales lifted one element of behavior change from sports, coaching, it forgot the other much more powerful one: practice. Yes, we know that salespeople hate practicing. But it works. In other occupations that require constant high performance, from performing arts to the military, repeated practice is the foundation of success. Embedding a culture of practice (before critical customer meetings and presentations) is a safe way to achieve big gains. How many customer visits have you been on where you winced as the salesperson did something that could have easily been corrected in a prior practice session? Practice sessions are also an easy way to leverage the power of peer feedback. Once a rigorous practice model has been established, the manager need not even be present.

Developing Culture

As the role of the sales manager evolves, one change that is beginning to take root is the need for managers to create a defined sales culture for their teams. While virtually every company has a defined set of values and a formal or informal culture, it is up to the manager to translate that into a meaningful set of expectations for salespeople.

Sales culture today has several components. First, it means connecting the work and achievements of salespeople to the mission of the larger organization. That means developing an identity and defining a purpose for the sales team that is more significant than simply achieving each year's numbers. It means articulating what your sales team is going to be best at, or what it will accomplish, or what it will be known for. Yes, salespeople are motivated in part by financial rewards, but it's not true, as some say, that they are "coin-operated." Like all other people, salespeople are driven by contributing to a larger good. It is up to the sales manager to define that larger good.

Second, the sales manager can create an environment in which particular behaviors, like preparation and practice, are valued. In companies where these behaviors are routine, salespeople are able to deliver higher quality more consistently. Valuing behaviors like preparation and practice means recognizing people for putting in the effort in advance of customer meetings, not only recognizing them for the outcomes of successful meetings. Other behaviors that can be incorporated into an intentional sales culture include integrity, transparency, fairness, and collaboration. Whatever values the sales manager holds in esteem should be emphasized, discussed openly, and recognized when demonstrated.

The Manager's Role in Selection

In Chapter 12, we outlined seven key behaviors that are required for salespeople to be successful in today's environment. When it comes to selecting new salespeople for the team, the sales manager should be using behavioral interviewing techniques to assess each candidate's capabilities in each of those seven areas. We also find that putting candidates through a role-play experience of preparing for and conducting a sales meeting can reveal strengths and gaps that might be hidden by simply asking questions alone.

Beyond the behavioral assessment, however, lies an equally important set of qualities to be explored. Those are the personal attributes of each candidate. Historically, we have found that studies of the qualities that make up great salespeople have jumbled together knowledge, behavior, and personal attributes. But we find it critical to separate those three categories. Knowledge is useful to separate from behavior because you can train for the two differently. Knowledge can be transmitted fairly effectively through e-learning, but behavior almost always requires face-to-face interactions to develop. Personal attributes cannot be taught at all. You must select for them.

We cannot claim to have done extensive psychometric research on the personality components of great salespeople. However, from working with dozens of top sales forces and studying the behavior of high performers, we can offer the following advice based on our observations of what we believe are critical personal attributes:

- **Proactivity.** Look for people eager to be at the front of the pack, leading the way. That means passivity and hesitation are deal breakers. Ask candidates about situations in which they were part of a group that faced a complex challenge, and explore their role in guiding the team forward in uncertain waters. Pay attention to how actively or passively they manage their role in the selection process. Do they look for opportunities to demonstrate their strengths while still showing respect for the process?

- **Accountability.** Ask about how the candidates set and accomplish goals. Do they own the goal, or do they feel that a target was handed to them? Identify situations in which the candidates were part of something that went wrong. What language do they use to describe the mistakes? Do they take ownership for the outcome and their contribution?

- **Curiosity.** Keep in mind that no amount of questioning skills training can substitute for natural curiosity. If the candidates come from outside your company, what kind of research have they done? What questions are they asking about your business? Are they curious about your company's goals and your personal interests and objectives? Or are their questions focused largely on their potential role and their own needs?

- **Honesty and integrity.** Screen for honesty and integrity. You cannot afford, and your customers do not want, people who take ethical shortcuts or are willing to mislead others to accomplish their objectives. If the customer does not trust the salesperson, there is no opportunity for the salesperson to build a relationship. Ask the candidates to describe difficult ethical situations they have encountered. What did they take into account in choosing how to proceed? Looking at the candidate's experience and what he or she tells you, what does your gut say? Do you have any doubts about this person's integrity?

- **Tenacity.** Look for people who persevere through difficult circumstances. Great salespeople cannot give up (or freeze up) when they encounter trouble. Trouble is a given on any complex journey. Find out about unexpected situations that the candidates have run into on the path to accomplishing a goal and how they responded. Watch how they respond if there are unexpected delays in the hiring process.

You are looking for curious people who can listen and then quickly articulate a compelling vision that customers will follow. Being more intentional about the kind of salesperson you are looking for can yield big results.

Conclusion—Embracing Change

In times of change from an X past to a Y future, it becomes even more critical for sales managers to develop their people in an intentional way. That means, in part, leveraging opportunities for salespeople to modify their behavior based on customer and peer feedback, since that is the most powerful form of feedback. It means demonstrating what great looks like, and it means establishing a culture that values preparation and practice. Of course, it also means selecting new members of the team in a thoughtful way, aligned to the vision of that future.

In times of X-to-Y change, it's natural for salespeople to feel the emotional effects of the uncertainty in their organizations. So it's critical, as a manager, to put your own oxygen mask on first, before helping others. In turbulent times, having plans (account, opportunity, etc.) is more critical than ever. The planning process should include having significant discussions of multiple scenarios, creating mental maps for potential outcomes, and reducing anxiety.

Today's world of rapid change requires sales managers to build environments where change is recognized as a positive. We've heard training professionals say that their people are experiencing "change fatigue" and that leadership should slow the pace of change. In our view, that is a recipe for stagnation and decline. In today's markets, change fatigue is no more realistic than "weather fatigue" would be. Change is a fact of life, and those that adapt to it will become champions of it rather than victims of it. Yes, change can be hard, but changing markets are filled with opportunity for those who can take advantage of new conditions and situations and who are not paralyzed by a romantic view of the past.

CHAPTER 16

Great Sales Management: Executing the Plan

Throughout the course of this book, we have documented the changing customer buying patterns that are reshaping the world of sales. Those dynamic conditions are creating longer sales cycles, higher volatility, and increased uncertainty, all of which make the life of a sales manager more difficult. How do sales managers respond to this roller-coaster environment they find themselves in today?

Typically, the sales managers we observe focus on ensuring high activity levels for their team. They drive more prospecting, more calls, and more proposals. They get more involved in big opportunities. Toward the end of the quarter, they apply super-human effort (and sometimes large discounts) to close deals. However, even when this approach works (and it doesn't always), it just sets them up to repeat the same behaviors the next quarter. It's a race that is not fun for any of the participants.

In early man, the stress hormone cortisol was released to mobilize all the body's resources in the face of a threat or predator. In today's world cortisol is released continuously in response to stressful conditions, making us feel anxious, ready for action, and restless even though we also feel tired. When sales managers face constant performance-related stress, their bodies are routinely filled with cortisol, and they are left feeling that they are being chased by a lion all day, every day.

How do great sales managers respond differently to the volatility and unpredictability that they face today? We see three differentiators among great sales managers, which we will explore in depth below. First, they have a different attitude. They act as if they own their business and the outcomes it produces, rather than as if they were a farmhand carrying out orders for others. Second, they have a different relationship with data. They constantly seek data, and they revise their approaches based on that data. Finally, they focus on a few critical priorities and metrics that will set them up for the short-term future, and they see their primary role as directing their team to align their focus similarly.

The Ownership Attitude

Great sales managers hold themselves accountable for their results. Not their teams, not their leaders. Not the otherworldly people in marketing, or the ornery people in pricing, or the constantly changing people in customer service, or the inward-focused people in supply chain. Themselves.

That means they make decisions in the interest of the business that will create the results for which they are accountable.

Not only does that attitude mean not blaming others; it also means not seeing themselves as order takers from above. They believe they own each decision themselves.

All of this is much harder than it sounds, as sales managers have suffered from years of being told to do this and then to do that, all while getting the reports done and solving that big customer problem, and getting the big deal closed by the end of the quarter, and don't forget coaching. Many don't feel in control of their destinies and frequently ask themselves, "Who am I going to disappoint today?" But those who are succeeding apply a few simple approaches.

First, they keep their eyes on the results they are charged with achieving. Everything they do and they have their teams do is measured through the filter of what will have the most impact on results. They look at salesperson activities and ensure that the emphasis is on those that will actually drive results. This might seem obvious, but in many organizations the prioritization of critical sales activities was done so long ago or by a set of people so removed from selling that there often is no more than unquestioned belief that links the measured sales activities to actual sales results. Sales managers with an ownership attitude are willing to challenge current practices with solutions that better serve the interests of customers, employees, and the organization.

Some sales managers ignore important stakeholders (e.g., pricing, marketing, or legal) or pay attention only to those with whom they have a personal relationship. It's understandable, given the number of competing pressures on a manager's time. But it's not effective. Other sales managers immediately respond to every internal request, making their jobs so internally focused that they lose sight of their customers. Great sales managers handle internal stakeholders as if they were shareholders. That is to say that all these different functions (not only pricing, marketing, and legal, but HR, customer service, engineering, supply chain, etc.) have a stake in the success of the managers and their teams. The managers' role with stakeholders is to effectively communicate their desired results and their priorities for achievement of those results. With clarity on results, great sales managers balance the competing requests from stakeholders rather than ignoring or overserving any of them. They prioritize actions and responses based on their goals, rather than allowing all their time to be absorbed by what seems most urgent.

The ownership attitude that great sales managers exhibit also applies to how they view data and reports. Next we'll explore how these great sales managers use data differently, as an outcome of this different mindset.

It's My Data

Great sales managers base their decisions on data. They do not think about "data" as one more report they need to produce for their boss (as many sales managers do) or simply as financial reporting or forecasting mechanisms for those above them, but rather they see the data as for themselves, to make better decisions. These great sales managers analyze the data, looking for patterns that might provide new insights or approaches, rather than just reviewing the variables or metrics that others focus on.

They complement this data with perspectives from multiple customers and prospects, talking to new people all the time, to expand their worldview. This qualitative research not only provides a different kind of insight than the data does; it also provides the fodder for the stories and examples that can be used to bring the data to life and drive behavior change.

Great sales managers are willing to change their minds based on new data. Whether it is new numbers, new customer feedback, or a colleague's compelling argument, they are willing to allow their personal point of view to evolve.

These great sales managers also have the confidence to know that there is more than one path to their results. Therefore, they don't become obsessed with one way of achieving those results. In times of fluidity, they instinctively know how important it is to remain agile. They are willing to experiment, based on what the quantitative and qualitative data is telling them, and they create a culture of experimentation that engages salespeople in constantly finding new ways to achieve their goals. That dynamic replaces the hopelessness of activity measurement with the hopefulness of innovation and creativity.

Focus on a Few

Great sales managers focus on just a few things. It could be a few priorities or a few metrics. These can change from time to time, but within a given performance period they are super-clear to their teams about what is important and what will be measured. That clarity of intent simplifies the chaotic world around them and makes it easier for their teams to perform.

People often ask us, "What is the right number of priorities or metrics to have?" but there is no magic number. The answer, though, is pretty straightforward: the fewer you have, the more likely you will be to achieve them. Five is better than nine. Three is better than five. You want the fewest priorities and the fewest measures but enough to achieve your goals.

We recently did some work for a major bank. In our discussions, we asked what metrics their relationship managers (salespeople) were measured on. As the people we were working with called out metrics, we flip-charted a list of 10 different measures. "How do the relationship managers balance all of these and know what to do?" we asked. "Column K," they responded with smiles. They explained that on the spreadsheet where all this is tracked, each metric is listed in a column, from A to J. Column K calculates a formula that weighs each of the measures differently. It's not possible, they laughingly admitted, to do the calculation in your head. "Everyone just refers to Column K!" What's more, from quarter to quarter the weights are changed based on current priorities, creating a constantly shifting state defined by announcements of "Everyone now to this side of the boat . . . now everyone to this side of the boat," which leaves their people unable to set priorities—and a bit seasick.

The list of 10 metrics we were provided at that bank was characteristic of what we typically see. Several of the metrics measured the same thing in microscopically different ways. Some focused on activity levels (e.g., number of client presentations), and some focused on outcomes (e.g., growth in new deposits), which in itself is not a bad idea, but the metrics were not grouped in a way that suggested a logic of how some led to others.

Great sales managers have figured out that the answer in these situations is to focus on very few metrics. That short list should include both lagging metrics (e.g., sales results, market share, margins) and leading-indicator metrics. These leading-indicator metrics, which we also refer to as in-process measures, can tell you if new behaviors are leading you to better results over time. There is a long list of potential in-process measures, and we have found that they need to be chosen very carefully. You have to determine what is truly correlated with future results in your company and in your industry, given the data tracking and reporting systems you have available to you. Below is a list of metrics that can be a starting point:

- In-process leading-indicator metrics

- Funnel (or pipeline) size

- Funnel velocity

- Conversion rates: funnel (or pipeline) stage to stage

- Win rate: percentage of opportunities won versus lost

- Sales cycle length (including time to a "no" decision, not just time to wins)

- Deal quality (e.g., lack of discounting)

- Number of new opportunities generated in a given period

- Accounts with high-quality account plans

- Ratio of individuals' funnel sizes to their quota targets

There are probably an infinite number of others. You will see that we have minimized the inclusion of pure activity metrics. We have consistently seen that, despite the popularity of doing so, measuring sales activity levels often drives the wrong outcomes. For instance, if you measure the number of meetings with customers or the number of proposals submitted, what you will get is a lot of meetings and a lot of proposals. Often those meetings and proposals are creating and responding to unqualified opportunities. You start seeing an increase in the size of the funnel but also an increase in the length of the average sales cycle, as the funnel gets filled with opportunities that will never close because they aren't real, or a decrease in the win rate because of opportunities that are not well suited to your value proposition.

As a starting point for a conversation, we find that two measures, funnel size and funnel velocity, are typically good leading indicators. Yes, both can have distortions, but they are fairly easy to track, and they show whether a particular change in behavior is having an impact. If you combine them with some measure of funnel quality (e.g., win rate or pricing adherence), you have a pretty good picture of what your future will look like.

The bottom line here is that people can only remember a few metrics. And salespeople need to be able to do in their heads the calculations that convert their performance numbers to their compensation and targets. Fewer metrics also increase individual accountability and contribute to a great perception of fairness—that everyone is being measured against the same criteria.

It is up to the sales managers to find the precious few metrics (lagging and leading) that are at the core of how they define performance. Then those managers need to refocus their team regularly on those measures, by asking questions like, "Will doing that help us improve our funnel size? Will it help us achieve our gross margin target?"

Keeping the team regularly focused on the right results—and the right priorities to achieve them—is best accomplished by applying a standard sales cadence across your team. That is actually not that complicated. It simply means a standard schedule of manager-rep interactions that are predictable and consistent.

The first step in deploying a sales cadence is to recognize that there are Y periods of activity. Certain interactions are best done:

- Annually

- Quarterly

- Monthly

- Weekly

- Daily

Your decision is to look at the following five types of activities and decide when each will be done:

- Performance management

- Funnel or pipeline management

- Opportunity planning

- Account planning

- Territory planning

For example, you may decide that on an annual basis there will be a performance review, and perhaps territory and account strategies will be created or updated. On a quarterly basis, you expect a business review for each salesperson's territory, and you will provide feedback on performance. On a monthly basis, you expect a detailed funnel review. On a weekly basis, you may want to be actively engaged in planning for specific opportunities, and you may be reviewing funnels at a high level. You may even want (particularly in an inside sales setting) to review certain call priorities or planned sales activities on a daily basis.

Your priority in conducting this cadence with the people on your team is to keep them focused on your small set of priorities for the current performance period. You should always return to the same small set of metrics on which they are measured. By following this focused approach, you will help your people tune out a lot of the noise that distracts from effective execution. You will also create a daily line of sight between each person's activities and the strategy you've created for your team, which not only drives focus but, perhaps more importantly, drives purpose. It reminds people why they are doing what they are doing and increases their motivation to succeed.

Conclusion—Focus on the Next Quarter

Here's a final thought to guide you in setting priorities. We can all bemoan the increasingly short-term focus of the companies we work for, driven in part by the quarterly expectations of investors. Nevertheless, it's the world we live in. Like many others, we believe a longer-term focus would be healthier and ultimately drive larger success, but that is often not feasible. So here's a reasonable middle ground. As a sales manager, focus not just on this quarter, but have a continuous bias toward making the decisions that will set your team up for the following quarter. Keeping your focus one quarter ahead will create a flywheel effect that continually accelerates success. It's also less stressful than feeling that lion chasing you every day.

CHAPTER 17

Great Sales Leadership

Not long ago, a wide-body Airbus 330 lost power in both its engines at an altitude of 39,000 feet over the South China Sea. Needless to say, the airplane began to glide downward. Passengers reported that this was felt as a gentle descent. The pilots controlled the descent while they reviewed the checklists created for just this sort of situation. Following the checklist, the crew was able to restart both engines within 10 minutes, by the time the plane was at 26,000 feet. Flight attendants then continued with meal service, and the plane landed at its intended airport a couple of hours later.

Now imagine the parallel situation in the world of sales. The team unexpectedly misses its targets by substantial amounts for two quarters in a row. What typically happens? First, people deny there's a problem. They attribute the performance to a temporary blip that will correct itself. Second, people argue about the cause, typically deflecting attention to things out of their control (the economy, a delay in a new product launch, a big change at a major customer, etc.). Finally, people debate the proper way to proceed, often arguing for vastly different courses of action.

Let's see if we can apply the lessons of aviation to this unfortunately common situation in the world of sales. In flight school, all pilots are taught rule #1: "No matter what happens, keep flying the plane." If the Airbus pilots panicked after losing both engines and became absorbed in their manuals, they could have lost control of their aircraft. Instead, one pilot focused on continuing to fly the plane, using the controls still available (wing flaps, stabilizer, etc.). The other pilot focused on the checklist for dealing with dual engine loss.

In sales, we sometimes see leaders become so distracted by the problem in front of them that they forget to keep flying the plane. As a result, the focus shifts away from customers and away from current opportunities, and more deals are lost, worsening the results. So the first step for sales leaders is to keep flying the plane, by keeping salespeople focused on their current business and opportunities.

Just like in the aircraft scenario, the next step is to stabilize the immediate situation and to hold off trying to solve for the underlying cause and future implications until there is more time. For a sales leader, that can mean analyzing the available data (the equivalent of the pilot's indicators). Is this an engine problem, a fuel problem, a software issue, a problem with the flaps? Quickly determine what is malfunctioning. Is it a problem in acquiring new customers? Is it a problem with existing accounts? Is the win-loss ratio changing? Are sales cycles getting longer? Are some salespeople continuing to be successful and others losing ground? What are competitors experiencing?

The next lesson is the checklist. What made the difference in the Airbus situation was a checklist. The situation of losing all engines, while rare, is a foreseen possible event in aviation.

Pilots are trained on how to respond, and a checklist ensures all steps are taken. It's not likely we'll have checklists created for all the problems that sales leaders are likely to encounter. But it is possible to apply a standard approach when problems are encountered:

- Talk to your salespeople. They are closest to the action. What do they say needs to be done?

- Talk to customers. Don't make assumptions or draw conclusions based on data or sales team suggestions without testing your ideas with customers.

- Form a narrative. Be able to explain what is happening and why. Admit you could be wrong and acknowledge that you might change your mind based on further data, but describe what you believe based on what you know today.

- Emphasize a very small number of simple actions to be applied repeatedly and consistently.

- Measure progress using leading indicators (as discussed in the previous chapter) to ensure that you have chosen the right actions to remedy the situation.

- Report progress, celebrating success and acknowledging where progress is not yet occurring, along with recognizing the lessons being learned and identifying further steps that need to be taken.

Finally, once things are stabilized, resume the in-flight meal service. What we mean is, return things to normality so that people can function and go about their business. The negative results may be the indicator of a need for a major change from X to Y, but that will take some time to figure out. In the meantime, keep people functioning.

For sales leaders, flying the plane means executing continuously toward their targeted results. We find that two areas of focus have the greatest impact on continuous execution, and both involve the leader defining what "great" looks like.

Defining a Clear, Compelling, Agile Future

The fundamental job for the sales leader is to define a picture of the future. Our recommendation is to use a fairly simple, three-step model to narrate a straightforward, memorable story:

1. **An explanation of the past.** Historically, what were the key success factors to selling in this market? What made us successful?

2. **An explanation of the present.** Which elements of the past approach stopped working in the last few years? Why? What changed in customer organizations? What changed in the competitive environment? What did our company and others do in response to these changes?

3. **An explanation of the future.** What emerging trends suggest that the present approach may not be viable for the long term? Are new market entrants applying a different business model or a different way for customers to buy? Is new technology creating a new set of offerings? Are we beginning to see emerging competitors with lower costs

of labor, lower costs of raw materials, or lower costs of capital? What strengths of our past and current state must we continue to maintain and invest in?

One of the benefits of a three-step story is that it places the current need for change in the context of past transformations and reinforces the need for continuous agility.

With this story in hand, sales leaders can then articulate a clear purpose, which takes the form, more or less, of a vision for Y and a vision for the interim XY period. "Our purpose is to be the best at Y, which is where our customers are headed, and we will get there by leveraging our historic strengths in X. We will move through a period of offering both X and Y, which will allow us to build our capabilities and make a smooth transition to the future." You simply replace X and Y in those sentences with whatever you have determined them to be.

That clear purpose will motivate the people on the sales force and reinforce their identity. They will know why they are taking on this major transformation and why the costs of change are worth it. The context story will help them understand the implications of not changing. Clarity on who you are and why you do what you do will drive the right behavior in ambiguous situations.

That well-communicated strategy must be matched with agile execution. The leader's role in setting the foundation for agile execution is to articulate two or three things that are the most important to you this year and what will likely be most important next year. Your direction to the members of the sales force, then, is to measure their activities, behaviors, and results by evaluating their contribution to those priorities. They should reallocate their time to ensure that those priorities are achieved.

A further approach to building agile execution is to change the focus of your communications. One element of your communications should include a report of what you are seeing in the customer and competitive environment. Continue to identify and highlight what is changing, and put those developments in the context of the story you built earlier.

Finally, it is worth noting that it is impossible for one person to drive transformation. You need a team to own pieces of the execution. Ideally that team includes most of your direct reports, but also stakeholders from other parts of the organization who will be key to your success. The more people co-owning the journey with you, the sooner you'll be successful.

Measuring the Distance to the Future

The most successful sales leaders are always assessing where they are in relation to their market. They begin by looking at their position in the market. Are they leading or following? How far ahead or behind are they? The best sales leaders do not just place themselves relative to the competition. Instead they think about where their customers are headed and how those customers are likely to buy in the future. Where is the sales leader's team in relation to those new buying patterns? Is the sales leader's company known in the market for creating the future? Or simply for being a solid legacy company? Are new market entrants changing the game?

These sales leaders then assess their offerings and way of selling. Is the core (X) business growing, or has it matured? Is there a Y business that needs to be nurtured? It's also worth looking at the X and Y offerings independently for a moment. How is each positioned in the market? Where is the competition relative to X and relative to Y? There are likely some different competitors for X and Y. Which ones are selling XY combinations in the market, and what kind of success are they having? How are the biggest customers in the market responding to X-to-Y change? Are they beginning to buy Y? Are they buying XY combinations?

Remember that X and Y can be about what you sell or how you sell. Is there a different way of selling that will be required soon or in the future? Are you seeing different groups of salespeople show success than you did in the past? Are they selling in a different way? Are your most successful salespeople now selling to different buyers than your organization did in the past?

These questions begin to map out a path toward sales transformation. While you would want to collect much more data before making critical decisions, the answers to the questions above indicate whether some level of sales transformation might be required and what the general direction might be. They begin to suggest what some of the alternative Xs and Ys might be for you to consider.

Assessing the Team and the Situation

Once you know where you are headed, it can be tremendously valuable to assess your team's capabilities. We are fans of robust approaches to assessment when they are custom built based on what truly drives success in your organization. Too many assessments are built on behaviors that defined great selling 20 or more years ago, in a company different from yours. Your company has a unique strategy, market position, way of working, and culture. You need to define "great" for your company in your current circumstances. Don't accept what someone else defined as great a long time ago in a galaxy far, far away.

Robust assessments can be time consuming and expensive. They are worth the investment, particularly when you are embarking on a major hiring campaign, as they will have the most validity and the strongest legal defensibility. However, often a sales leader does not have the time or budget to apply a comprehensive approach. In these cases, it is significantly better than nothing to deploy a simplified assessment process, as long as it is customized to your business. If you treat the results as directional (rather than prescriptive or scientific), you can get a lot of value out of this back-of-the-envelope approach.

It all begins with your definition of X and Y, and as we've underscored throughout this book, XY. Then you can answer the following questions:

- Which skills from selling X translate to selling Y?

- What new skills are essential to sell Y?

- What is required when people are selling both X and Y? What are the essential XY capabilities? (For instance, collaboration typically becomes more important as the use of team selling increases during the XY period.)

The next step is assessing your customers' readiness:

- Will your customers accept your sellers as experts in Y?

- Are the buyers changing?

- Are the customers' buying processes changing?

You can then assess your selling process, coverage model, and compensation:

- What changes need to be made to efficiently drive buying?

- Is your current way of assigning salespeople to customers sufficient to support selling Y?

- What needs to happen in the XY period that is different from what will ultimately be needed to sell a pure-Y offering?

- What should you measure? How should it be reported?

- Does compensation need to change?

- Are certain support functions redundant or no longer necessary?

- What new sales tools are required to enable the team to be effective, and which ones do you need to stop using?

- To what extent do you need Y experts to support salespeople in moving from selling X to selling XY and Y?

Conclusion—A Vision for XY

Remember this above all: the job of the sales leader is to define the vision not just for the Y future but for the XY transition stage as well. And all of that must be done with a genuine respect for X because you need people to continue to sell X as you make the transition to Y.

PART 5

Conclusions

CHAPTER 18

Pivotal Moments

S ales transformation can be such an overwhelming thought that many people prefer to avoid the term, which is fine. But it doesn't have to be overwhelming. Let's make it easier.

Five key moments determine whether a sales transformation will be successful.

Moment #1: Recognition

Is it time for a sales transformation? Only the sales leader can make that evaluation, and of course any decision to embark on a major change must be assessed in concert with the larger executive team. In statistics, there are what are known as Type I and Type II errors. Type I errors are false-positives. In this situation, it would mean deciding that a sales transformation is needed when it really isn't. Type II errors are false-negatives: deciding that a sales transformation is not needed when it really is. We haven't seen many false-positives in the decisions to embark on sales transformations. Much more common are the Type II errors, failing to embark on a sales transformation early enough, or at all.

While we don't have statistics to prove it, we find that new sales leaders are disproportionately likely to initiate a sales transformation. Perhaps you can say that they are looking to make their mark, but more realistically, we think it is that new sales leaders are not locked into legacy thinking, so they look at everything with fresh eyes.

In Chapter 6, we provided a list of developments that might indicate the need for a sales transformation. Here is that list again:

- Consistently flat or declining revenues

- Activity from competitors (especially new entrants) that threatens the future of the existing revenue base

- The approaching obsolescence of a key product or the introduction of a radically new product

- Quickly changing customer expectations

One way to test whether a sales transformation is necessary is to try defining X and Y in several different ways. It's a worthwhile exercise. Start with defining what Y might be. Think about new technology, new selling channels, radically new products, new buyers, new approaches to buying or selling, and new payment structures. For each Y you create, identify the parallel X state that defines where your company is today. Which of those X and Y pairs do you think is central to what is happening in your market? Do you believe that the shift is real, is significant, and is likely? If so, it's time to move on initiating a sales transformation.

If you're a salesperson or a sales manager, obviously you can't make the decision to embark on a sales transformation. However, you can alert your sales leaders to the indicators that make you believe a major change will be necessary. Even if it falls on deaf ears initially, it may trigger a response when added to what others are saying. In any case, it's your obligation to point things out, in a manner, of course, that is constructive. And if your sales leader is unreceptive, you can still experiment with changes in the way you sell personally, or in the way you manage your team, that begins to test a new approach. Many sales transformations actually begin when one team starts delivering performance that stands out from what the rest of the organization is doing.

Moment #2: Communicating the Vision

As we've said repeatedly, it's the sales leader's job to create a vision for Y along with a vision for the XY transition. Doing so requires a clearheaded assessment of how salespeople, and their customers, are likely to respond to the change. What is most critical is the recognition that a transition period will be required. The hope you express for that period is that people will begin to (1) sell XY combinations to customers, (2) sell X and Y separately but selling both to the same customer organizations, and (3) sell X and Y to different customers, selling X to some and Y to others (which essentially means beginning to sell Y on its own).

Once you have the vision, you need to communicate it. That must be done in a way that respects the past. It's worth celebrating what has made the company great and what will not change.

It is also worth recognizing what contributed to past success but will need to change. Most importantly, you need to show that continuing to sell X is still highly valued. Not all your salespeople will shift to selling even XY overnight, and you don't want to demotivate those sellers. In most cases, the market for Y will not outpace the market for X for several years, so you can't afford to signal a need for reduced performance in the X space. You have to continue to support the X business while you build the XY and Y businesses.

Remember that as you introduce Y and XY, you probably won't be met with thundering applause. People often fear change, and initially the natural response is to deny the need for change. You have to repeat the message consistently for a bewilderingly long period of time, in different venues, using different media and approaches.

Moment #3: Recognizing Early Success

In the beginning stages, as we've noted, you'll have some people naturally selling Y, and you'll have many others beginning to experiment successfully with selling XY. You want to celebrate both those groups, as they are critical to your future performance. When early success proves durable, you may want to put the high performers in those groups into more visible roles. Those can be formal positions, or they can be informal roles where they are mentoring and advising others in the organization. Those folks are your ambassadors, and they will help you carry your message to many more people. When the message is transmitted by peers, it will be amplified. Take good care of those people.

Part of recognizing success in the early stages also means, counterintuitively, recognizing failure. The XY transition phase is never easy, and we said in Chapter 14 that humility combined with a mindset of experimentation is required. Celebrate the successful experiments, but also celebrate the unsuccessful ones because you've all learned something that will help you in the future. If you instead create the misimpression that a failed experiment is not valued, you will discourage people from experimenting.

In the early stages, you also want to entice X sellers to want to be part of the next group to experiment with XY. So, again, while you continue to recognize the importance of X, you want to make a big deal out of those X sellers who have begun to see success with XY. You may choose to invite teams into selling XY in stages, making it a somewhat exclusive club, rather than expecting everyone to adopt it at once, which in reality won't happen anyway.

Moment #4: Navigating the Second Stage

Back in Chapter 2, we reported that Stage 2 is the critical moment that determines success or failure in an X-to-Y transformation. If you recall, Stage 2 begins when you move from having just a few early adopters of Y and XY in Stage 1 to the point where half of your sales force is now selling XY or Y (with the vast bulk in the XY stage). We see many change efforts begin to fail at this stage, and this is where many are abandoned (leading to the salesperson complaint about "flavor-of-the-month" initiatives).

Stage 2 is the tipping point for sales transformations, and it's worth investing all the energy you can to make sure it goes right.

Don't be afraid to break Stage 2 into smaller phases. Phasing the rollout can enable you to learn lessons early and apply them later.

One critical way to improve the chance for success is to be deliberate about which populations are invited into each phase of Stage 2. Deploy pilot groups. Find the sales managers and teams that are motivated and have the needed capabilities. Oversupport them with training, feedback, resources, and recognition. Whatever the cost of those support mechanisms, it will be far less than that of hiring a new Y sales force. Later you'll be able to determine which support structures are required as you continue the rollout through the rest of the organization in Stages 3 to 5, which, by the way, begin to take care of themselves if you get Stage 2 right.

Moment #5: Spotting Z

By the time you get to Stage 5 of the distribution curve, all your reps are selling Y. But wait. Just when you thought it was safe to take a breath, now is the time when Z emerges, and you have to begin the whole process over again, defining the vision for Z and for the YZ transition.

If you've chosen Y well, Z won't derail you for some time. The mistake we often see is that once the recognition of market change begins to be valued, people begin seeing it everywhere. Everyone has a theory about what's next. Some will see potential rewards in recognition in spotting Z first. Others will use a false identification of Z to argue that the X-to-Y transformation is misguided. Your job is to keep people focused. Yes, numerous possible Zs will appear on the horizon, but until they exceed the thresholds we outlined at the beginning of this chapter, everyone needs to focus on the X-to-Y game.

Perhaps the best news about Z is that it's easier the second time. You've been down this road before, and you know what you need to do. Your confidence is greater, and you have great stories to tell. It's the beginning of another fantastic journey.

CHAPTER 19

Summary of
Selling Vision

This book is about sales. It is also about change management. In fact, in many respects, sales today is essentially change management. The advice that underlies this book is to define not just the future vision but also the transition state, and to place your execution focus there.

Part 1 of this book introduced a new logic for thinking about change and sales transformations. In Part 2, we examined how sales transformation needs to accommodate the fast change that is continuously occurring in customer organizations. In Part 3, we looked at the perspective of salespeople and how they can sell change to their customers who are also going through transformations. In Part 4, we offered a script for how sales leaders and sales managers can change the way selling works in their organizations. Part 5 began with conclusions about five pivotal moments in sales transformations, and now we end with a summary of *Selling Vision's* most important messages.

The New Logic

We offered a simple model of sales transformation, where a company is in a shift from selling a lot of X and a little bit of something new called Y . . . to a lot of Y and much less of the legacy X offering. We noted that X and Y can be what you sell or how you sell.

The conventional wisdom says that the leader's goal is to get more of the X salespeople to sell Y as fast as possible. But salespeople, like other people, resist change. (Actually, first they deny the need for change; then they resist it.) Most salespeople who are told and taught to start selling Y revert fairly quickly to selling X, which is what made them successful in the first place. Sales leaders become frustrated by their inability to drive the shift they need. They consider hiring Y salespeople to replace the X salespeople.

A better way is to recognize that transformation is not a binary event, where you turn off X and turn on Y, as if there were a switch. The salespeople who truly migrate to selling Y go through a period of selling both X and Y at the same time or selling a blended solution that includes both X and Y to their customers. The recognition of the XY transition state is the key to understanding sales transformation. The most critical element of making a sales transformation successful is describing what the XY transition state looks like and how to sell either X and Y simultaneously or XY combinations.

For salespeople, seeing change through an X → XY → Y lens (as opposed to an X → Y lens) reduces ambiguity, prevents weariness, and limits shock. The key initial focus of salespeople should be to (1) expand their network of buyers, (2) learn to make the case to their customers that supports XY buying, and (3) adapt their approach depending on how competitors have positioned themselves.

The impossible job of the sales manager only gets more difficult during periods of sales transformation. Sales leaders must embrace the vision for Y and articulate what XY looks like for their team, setting new priorities that support the XY transition. The first job of the sales leader and sales manager is to paint a vision not only for the Y future but also for the XY transition period.

A Change in Buying

Customers are going through X-to-Y transitions themselves. As they do so, they are questioning their own judgment, dealing with new stakeholders, and managing through ambiguity. The best salespeople help their customers on those journeys.

In fact, the pace of change is becoming so fast in customer organizations that it is creating turbulence that is disrupting buying decisions. As customers work to avoid risk, they are engaging more stakeholders and postponing decisions. Responding successfully to these situations, the best salespeople adapt their approach to recognize the types of buyers they are dealing with, and particularly whether those people are trying to maximize gains or minimize losses.

The current environment of fast change is creating periodic stalls in the execution of strategic initiatives in customer organizations. When purchases are linked to these strategic initiatives, the buyers go into what we call a decision vortex. Nothing happens, and no news is available. The decision vortex can then send the buying cycle backward or accelerate it forward.

Customers generally are going through a transition from buying products and solutions to buying accelerators of their business results. Outside of commodity purchases, customers want salespeople to focus their discussions on the business results that the customers need to achieve, not the product features they seek or even the specific problems they need to resolve. Customers report that few salespeople are selling this way, but when they do, the customers buy more, even at higher prices, because the value that is created is worth it. We call the difference between what customers seek and what salespeople typically provide a "value gap." That value gap is part of what is driving longer sales cycles, greater discounting, more frequent customer churn, and slower acquisition of new customers.

Selling Change

Customers today seek salespeople with "navigation" skills, that is, the ability to guide the customers on the journey to their destination. They seek salespeople who understand their industry terrain, can chart new trails based on their individual priorities, and know when to take a shortcut and when it is best to take the long way around. Navigation skills involve identifying the customer's destination, clarifying the path to that destination, and assuming responsibility for measuring progress.

The behaviors required for selling in a way that accelerates a customer's business results include:

- Demonstrating customer understanding

- Planning for each customer interaction, asking questions that get deep inside the customers' view of their business and what creates value for them

- Engaging the customer in co-creation activities to build a solution together

- Advancing the customers through their buying process

- Managing opportunities, accounts, and territories and collaborating with others in the selling company on behalf of the customer

Key account managers have an additional set of required behaviors for success in today's environment, the two most important of which are dynamic business acumen and business-case agility. Prospecting activity can be kick-started by focusing first on what the salesperson can do to serve the customers before trying to sell to them.

Getting customers out of decision vortices means recognizing that each vortex is really a prioritization challenge. The salesperson can provide tools and insights to help the customers better assess and establish those priorities, reducing doubt and uncertainty. One tool the salesperson can leverage is explaining the $X \rightarrow XY \rightarrow Y$ model to customers and helping them to define their own Y and XY visions.

Changing Selling

Current expectations for sales managers are not in sync with what is realistic or possible. We expect a significant reshaping of the sales manager role over the next decade. In the meantime, the best sales managers must strive to adequately balance the needs of their customers, team, and company, not overfocusing on any one area.

To succeed in today's environment, sales managers should think about their roles as falling into three categories. *Leading people* means communicating vision and cascading strategy; demonstrating executive presence; serving as the voice of the customer; and acting with a humble and experimental attitude. Sales managers must show that they authentically value the X business, the XY business, and the Y business. *Developing people* means—not "coaching"—but rather offering feedback, modeling the right behaviors, co-selling with reps, and creating a routine of practice. It also means creating an intentional sales culture, using better methods to select new team members, and creating an environment that values change. *Executing the plan* means taking ownership for the business and the outcomes the sales managers are achieving, basing decisions on quantitative and qualitative data, focusing their teams on a few, clear priorities, and deploying a predictable sales cadence.

Sales leaders are responsible for flying the plane. That means establishing the vision for the Y and XY futures. It also means providing the narrative that describes the journey that the sales force will be on, a narrative that acknowledges and appreciates the past while articulating the future. Sales leaders must enable their teams for agile execution by measuring only what will impact their top priorities for the performance period. The responsibilities of sales leaders include assessing their marketplace and team against what will be required for success in the Y world as well as in the XY transition stage.

Pivotal Moments

Five key moments determine whether a sales transformation will be successful: (1) recognizing in a timely way that a major change is needed, (2) communicating the vision for Y and XY while continuing to appreciate X, (3) recognizing early success, (4) navigating the stage when the majority of salespeople are selling XY or Y, particularly the early part of that stage, and (5) recognizing the appearance of Z, which triggers the next sales transformation.

Acknowledgments

The ideas that form the basis of this book have been triggered by our work with our clients and colleagues. We are incredibly grateful for the ways they challenge us to create new ideas, deepen our research, and inspire new ways of selling. They also make all our work exciting and fun.

We are especially appreciative of the dozen successful sales leaders around the world who generously provided their time and thinking in extended interviews.

Index

About the Authors

Lou Schachter leads the Global BTS Sales Practice, a team of 50 around the world, and drives research and intellectual property development. He works with clients such as Salesforce.com, Toyota, Citizens Bank, and Schindler, building great sales forces through innovative customer engagement models and helping leaders, managers, and sellers *See* sales behaviors from the customer's point of view. His deep global experience gives him the ability to help leaders shape their sales forces in markets all over the world.

He is passionate about moving the science of sales to the next level, looking for unconventional wisdom and challenging common sense that has become outdated. Lou is a true student of sales and all that has been written on it over the years.

Before joining the BTS team, Lou had a long career in sales for professional services firms. His experience includes selling to Fortune 500 companies, small businesses, and large government institutions. He also helped lead the fast growth of a specialized communications firm. Earlier in his career, he was an investment banker.

Lou is the coauthor of the book *The Mind of the Customer: How the World's Leading Sales Forces Accelerate Their Customers' Success*, which was published by McGraw-Hill in 2006.

Lou graduated from the Wharton School of the University of Pennsylvania. When not on airplanes, he lives in Los Angeles, with his partner, Wayne.

Rick Cheatham leads the U.S. Sales Practice for BTS. He works with clients such as Google, Accenture, Metlife, and IBM to drive their sales efforts into the future. Rick leads a team of over 20 consultants and conceptualizes many of the BTS solutions deployed in the United States.

He is passionate about making work a place that salespeople come to be successful, is totally pragmatic and experienced in getting results through being a purpose-driven leader, and is able to maintain an uncommon balance between vision and how things really get done.

Prior to coming to BTS, Rick was a sales leader for both regional and global account teams. Ultimately he led the sales force of a $1 billion business unit through a restructuring and shift in how they sold. That experience has shaped his thinking on how organizations can change what and how they sell faster and more effectively.

Rick lives in Austin with his wife, Jen, and four kids.

About BTS

The BTS Sales Practice partners with the most successful sales forces in the world, providing consulting, training, and technology to give salespeople the experiences and skills they need to do the best work of their lives. The BTS approach combines proprietary global sales research, clients' organizational wisdom, and insights uncovered together, to design simulations and training that are executed upon in the field using on-the-job tools.

BTS is a global professional services firm headquartered in Stockholm, Sweden, with some 450 professionals in 32 offices located on 6 continents. Among the clients of the BTS Sales Practice are Autodesk, BBVA Bancomer, BlueScope Steel, Chevron, Cisco, Ericsson, Google, Hewlett-Packard, IBM, Johnson & Johnson, KPMG, Microsoft, Nike, Oracle, Pfizer, Salesforce.com, SAP, Schindler, Sodexo, Standard Bank, Toyota, Twitter, UCB, UPS, and VMware.